BRITISH SOLDIER IN INDIA

The Letters of Clive Branson

INTERNATIONAL PUBLISHERS, NEW YORK

CONTENTS

Introduction

BY HARRY POLLITT

It is an honor to write an introduction to the letters that Clive Branson wrote from India. They paint an unforgettable picture that, I am sure, will rouse many people to anger and to action.

Who was Clive Branson? To know this man is to gain added understanding from what he has written.

The son of an army officer, he was born in India, in 1907—oddly enough in the little town of Ahmednagar to which he was to return 35 years later. As a baby he was brought back to England and went later to a boys' preparatory school, and from there to a public school (Bedford Grammar School). While a boy he showed great talent for drawing, and after he left school he went to study at the Slade School of Art. He was a prolific painter, and by the age of 23 had already exhibited two paintings in the summer exhibition of the Royal Academy. From the age of 20 onward he did a great deal of serious reading, starting with Volume One of Marx's *Capital,* and, after a brief sojourn in the I.L.P.* he joined the Communist Party in 1932. From then on he threw himself heart and soul into the working class movement and temporarily gave up painting altogether. He used to say that to be able to paint one must first learn about life. It was not until five years later that he again allowed himself time for painting, and began to exhibit once more, this time at the Lefevre Galleries. But by this time the Spanish war had broken out, and Clive could not rest until he had volunteered for service with the British Battalion of the International Brigade. In almost his first battle he was captured and spent eight months in a Franco concentration camp. On his return from Spain at the end of 1938 he organized the International Brigade Convoy, toured the

* Independent Labor Party.—*Ed.*

7

country, collecting over £5,000, which was used to send food and medical supplies out to Spain.

After the outbreak of the present war, while continuing his political work, he nevertheless spent a number of months painting very intensively, because, as he said, "it may be my last chance." He painted mainly the life in Battersea, where he lived, the workers in the streets, the events of the blitz. Some of these paintings were subsequently shown at an exhibition organized by the Artists' International Association.

In 1941 he was called up, and became a member of the Royal Armored Corps. A year later, he was drafted to India, and on February 25, 1944, was killed in action on the Arakan Front during the fighting for the Ngankedank Pass.

Such are the bare outlines of Clive's life. What of his work in the labor movement?

Clive was one of those who came to Communism, not because of personal experience of, and bitterness against, capitalism, but because of a profound intellectual conviction that it is a very wrong system which cannot be justified by any logic or reason.

He was one of those who endear themselves to all who come in contact with them, because of his untiring fight for social justice, and the boundless enthusiasm with which he carried on the struggle. He was able to inspire others to hate poverty and fight to remove it, to hate ugliness and see beauty. By his death the movement has lost not only an active member, but a wise counsellor, and one who never asked others to do what he was not prepared to do himself.

He was not only a brilliant speaker and organizer, but also did more than his share of what is sometimes called "the donkey work." Nothing was too much for him: selling the *Daily Worker* at Clapham Junction, house to house canvassing, selling literature, taking up local issues, and getting justice done—all those little things which go to make up the indestructible foundations of the labor movement.

He allied all this with serious educational work, and there are few local labor organizations in Battersea which do not remember the way in which he could make difficult subjects easy to understand.

His finest qualities were, however, shown in Spain when for many months he suffered the horrors of a Franco concentration

8

camp. His bearing, his advice and example were of tremendous assistance to those who were with him. One of his comrades wrote of this period in Clive's history:

"In any difficult time, Clive was always cheery, putting forward what we should do, and helping to educate others in order to use the time usefully. He was one of the most popular and most respected among the British prisoners."

After he joined the Royal Armored Corps, he proved himself a model of efficiency in mastering every aspect of armored warfare. He was repeatedly recommended for promotion, which might have been quicker in coming had it not been for the political prejudices which die so hard at the War Office. As it was, he held the rank of troop sergeant at the time of his death.

When he was sent overseas to India, as his letters show, he was quick to adapt himself to the new life. He gained new impressions, thoughts and ideas. He was enraged at the suffering and exploitation he saw. And through this he seemed to have acquired a new giant stature, a new command of language, and a love of India and its citizens which is one of the loveliest and most unforgettable features of his letters.

Written to his wife, these letters have a message for us all. You will read them for yourselves. They will make you angry and they will make you sad. They will make you see new colors and shades, an unimaginable suffering and a truly heroic grandeur, extraordinary nobility and equally extraordinary bestiality. It is a vivid and many-sided picture which Clive wanted to record in painting, and which, we may be sure, he would have executed with feeling and sincerity. As it is, we can capture from his letters something of the beauty which he saw.

Now he has gone. One of his mates, who was with him when he was killed in Burma, wrote home after his death:

"He now lies buried somewhere among the green-covered hills, but he has left us a high idea of the meaning of human dignity and the immortality of life.

"Our new humors and reversed outlooks are monuments to his

9

mental virility. It now remains for us to honor him and justify the risks he freely encountered."

This is indeed a noble tribute. What can we do to prove that we appreciate it?

I think that these letters are a challenge to every one of us. Let us read, again and again, that moving passage which gives almost his first impression after landing in India, when, writing of certain Britishers, he says:

"They treat the Indians in a way which not only makes one tremble for the future, but makes one ashamed of being one of them."

And let us remember, in reading this, that we have it in our power to remove this shame, that it is urgent to do so in the interests not only of the Indian people, but of the hundreds of thousands of British troops out there, whose fight against Japan is all the harder because we refuse to enable millions of Indian people to cooperate fully with us in the common struggle against fascism.

Let us remember, too, that liberty, like war and peace, is indivisible. And let us demand the same democratic rights for the Indian people that we claim for ourselves. Let us demand the right of these people to elect their own government. And, above all, let us help to relieve the famine, the ravages of which are so movingly described by Clive Branson, the black death of which he was one of the first to send news to this country, and which, he warned us, as other experienced observers have warned us, may take a greater toll in coming days than it did ever in the past, when bureaucratic inefficiency and heartless profiteering made that land of love into a jungle.

I am proud that Clive Branson was a member of the Communist Party. What inspired him has inspired many others, who have worked and sacrificed their lives, not only to defeat fascism, but to help the people forward toward Socialism. This alone, they knew, can transform poverty into plenty, war into peace, idleness into productive labor, and give new life to every artistic and cultural development in our time.

10

Part I: With the Regiment

May, 1942. Bombay

So it is India! I have arrived very fit, and in good spirits. On the boat I ended by giving many lectures on the International Brigade and found many friends. Although I have only been in India a little time there is one problem which hits you in the face—the life of the peasantry; and, in Bombay, the housing. But Oh, what a people this is for painting! I shall make many small notes and studies for pictures when this bloody business is over. Gad, Sir—when I was in Poona in '42. . . .

May 31, 1942. From Gulunche, Nr. Poona

A great deal has happened since my last letter. On landing we had a few hours to ourselves in Bombay. I went up to what looked like an Indian student (he was one) and asked him to show me where were the bookstalls so that I could get a book on Hindustani. I could not get the book as I had no Indian money, but I had a long talk with him.

We went by train from Bombay to a camp outside Poona. Everyone was filled with amazement at the appalling conditions in which the people live—this has been the subject of many very lively discussions since; not always by any means with the same or correct conclusions drawn, but without the slightest divergence of opinion on the basic fact that, after 175 years of imperialism in India, the conditions are a howling disgrace. For this reason, and its reactions on our own immediate future (and present), the slogan among the British Other Ranks* of "India for the Indians" is universally popular.

Of course, the problem for us is far more complicated than this. Naturally, the practical nearness of actual fighting with the Japs, the successes of the enemy, and the far distance we are from home, creates the elementary desire in all of us (except in the minds of

* Enlisted men.—*Ed.*

11

those insane fools who look upon war as a sport, good fun, etc.) for some miraculous ending to the war. As, of course, in the army *nothing* is done to explain things to the lads, one is almost daily called upon patiently to explain and explain why action out here is important, what our attitude to the natives and to Indian politics should be, etc. There is a deep-rooted tendency for the lads to treat the Indians in the traditional way, but daily contact with the native soldiers and civilians in the camp, sympathy for the mass poverty in the surrounding country, and the disgusting snobbishness of the Anglo-Indians both to the Indians and to the newly arrived British soldiers (in great contrast to the wonderful reception we got in Cape Town from the South African whites) is quickly teaching them the reality of our position.

We have now settled in to our camp. Conditions are not what I had hoped for at all. We are under canvas with beds, sheets. A laundry boy takes in washing at 1 anna* an article and returns it clean the same day. A tea boy brings round hot tea many times a day. The food is excellent. We get fruit in plenty. We sleep all afternoon. It is very hot, but heat, dryness and plenty to drink is quite a pleasant combination—it suits me, anyway. I have got the job of rations corporal which lets me go into a small railway town every day where I get a chance of learning by practice to speak Hindustani.

In my letters from the boat I spoke much of guerrilla fighting being the key to the successful defense of India. My real contact with this country convinces me even more of this; the mass, dense basis of the peasantry; the structure of the terrain; the food and water problem (practically impossible to solve on any large scale in modern warfare by the old system of army machinery alone) are things which one has seen, as well as the poor roads—now a question being dealt with at length in moving speeches in Bombay after years of increasing neglect by the authorities. A great historian of the nineteenth century—I have forgotten his name—once said that history repeats herself according to formula. First she enacts the drama, then she repeats with a farce. China is the drama—is India to be the farce?

My daily trip for rations has given me the idea for a scheme of

* An anna is worth about two cents.—*Ed.*

12

large wall-paintings illustrating, for instance, "Road building" in different countries—a scheme of decoration suitable for some large hall in a Ministry of Transport. What dignity the women laborers here in India give to the very primitive making of a country lane! I shall make some sketches of this job here on the spot as soon as I can speak the language better (providing, of course, I get the C.O.'s permission to draw!). In any case the scene has impressed me so deeply that I shall never forget its essentials. This country is giving me a new color sense. The other evening the sun was just setting making the whole sky a brilliant hard yellow. A laborer came past, his skin a brown black; round his head the folds of gleaming white cloth. The road, the dry earth, a pale mauve with strips of lemon-green sugar patches. No shadows—the light in the shaded parts being too rich in color to look different. This is a very simplified description, but a few months out here will improve my ability to see and record these new color relationships based on green and silver, platinum and mauve (this is the key to the painting of an Indian's head, and not black and white as perhaps with that of the Negro).

During supper I read a copy of the *Times of India*. It is evident that this question of a home guard is bothering the authorities. A report speaks of the Poona Civil Guard (the official outfit) and its activities, which include A.R.P., Lathi training (!) and police duties! It is not to be wondered at that it has only 200 members and that the masses won't (or cannot?) join up. A paper the other day solemnly stated that the main reason for not allowing the formation of a mass home guard was the inability to supply arms. Wonderful, isn't it? When the most innocent child should know that a guerrilla band's chief immediate task is *to arm itself by taking arms from the enemy* (as the tribesmen do in India at our expense at the moment). But more, the Chinese Eighteenth Route Army is *organized on this basis*. With every two men going into action, armed, there is one unarmed whose job it is to get hold of any equipment found either on fallen Japs or Chinese.

We have all noted the decisions of the Labor Party Conference —things are moving. But how very, very much we long to hear of the second front being started. It is almost dark so I will end this letter.

Little has happened since my last letter. I have seen one copy of the *Times of India* with a review of world opinion on the Soviet Pact including a statement by the chairman of the Congress.* His line is that, since the Pact is based on the Atlantic Charter and since the Atlantic Charter is not applicable to Indian independence, then Russia, too, has deserted the cause of freedom. Having analyzed the prospects thus, he turns on the Indian Communists with the question: "How can you say this is a peoples' war against Fascism?" Of course, he thereby shows his fear of the Indian masses, for it must be clear to any realist that peoples' wars are based on certain basic facts (prerequisites is the term we used to use) and even then it is not a peoples' war unless one passes from the stage of words by parties to deeds by the people. Here, so far as Congress is concerned, the leaders don't want to rouse the masses —but there are times in history when what happens and what leaders want are very different.

I had an amusing interview with an officer today. The conversation went as follows (much abbreviated):

He: Well, Branson, I want to thank you for your work on the rations, blah, blah, blah. No doubt the new Lt. Quartermaster will have you in mind if he wants a job done, etc.

Me: I don't want a job like that again, etc. I want to get some training. I want very badly to be a soldier.

It shook him all right, and perhaps it will result in my being put in charge of a fatigue party whose job it is to line up the blades of grass as they come up out of the earth since the rain began.

For the rain has indeed changed things. Roads become either blocked where they crossed river beds (normally dry)—previously serviceable tracks become mires, and the earth goes a deep purple with very green vegetation. Lizards, scorpions, and ants are driven into the open. A brilliant claret velvety beetle appears, and gigantic croaking frogs, bright yellow green.

I am continually struck by the extraordinary dignity of the little girls out here. I shall never forget one tiny wee tot walking by a field. She walked along, bolt upright. She had a turquoise blue dress (blouse-skirt, European kind), jet black hair, and dark face

---

* All-India Congress.—*Ed.*

14

and, behind her, brilliant, luscious green stalks of young sugar springing up and curving their new yellow emerald leaves over just above her head.

These last few days I have been suffering from an "upset tummy" which has not improved my temper when dealing with those bloody idiots in the regular army who want to indulge in abuse of the Indians. They treat the Indians in a way which not only makes one tremble for the future but which makes one ashamed of being one of them. Really, some of the most ignorant men here are to be pitied. They joined the regular army to get away from family trouble in Blighty. They never write home, they try to suppress all feelings about Blighty, they vent their own misfortunes on any hapless and helpless Indian, and they look upon army life as a scramble (all against all) for good jobs. The art of war, the character of this war, the outcome of the war outside of India just does not concern them: *they dare not let themselves be concerned* for fear of burning homesickness that smoulders beneath their simulated toughness. I have had the chance of talking to a few—My God, what *hideous* lives they lead. Eternally on the scrounge for petty gain; eternally feeling they are being swindled by the paymaster, by the canteen, the shopkeeper, etc., and therefore ready always to swindle someone else; disunited by the bitterness of life and yet united by their common fear of life and common hatred of the individual or persons to whom they attribute at the moment their exile from humanity.

The other morning I woke up from a dream that I had been walking 'round a picture gallery (I dream this so often) and came across a large picture of a man painting in a field. I looked at it and thought to myself, "I remember painting that." But I was doubtful, so I looked closer to find "Dona Torr" on the bottom left hand corner. I dream a lot these days, mainly due, I think, to the utter mental stagnation of my waking life.

Today, now that the regiment has come, everything is humming. The new Sergeant Major has taken over with the usual announcement, "If . . . to the guard room." There is one thing which no one in authority seems to understand at all—that *we want to get on with the job*—we are *not* peace-time soldiers, and it is not we who prevent things getting done but the persistent peace-time pace and con-

15

ceptions of the middle leadership. One of the officer's batmen* tells
me they have carpets down in their tents. We who have come out
here recently are longing to get down to work. We got the news
two days ago of a breach in the Sevastopol defenses. I hope this
isn't too serious—when *are* we going to open the second front?

The sky today is that of a fine English summer day, but one
misses the great elms with their leaves piled up like banks of cloud.
There is so much light, too, that one never gets those resonant
contrasts of dark shadow and graduated light of Rembrandt and
Constable. The only real darkness other than night is to be
found in the homes of the people, and there the contrast is one of
color rather than tone (as in Van Gogh's Potato Eaters).

Two things have just happened which stagger one in their
contrast. Tobruk has fallen, and we have been ordered to polish
all brasses on all our equipment. How much longer are we, the
English race, going to put up with such humiliation from creatures
whose only right to leadership is the Divine Right supposed to have
rolled from the scene of history along with Charles' head? We
now hear that *sergeants* are to have batmen!

. . . Since I wrote the above, a new program has been put up
which promises that from next week on we are going to be really
busy, which is very heartening. Many of us are so longing to get
on to the job so as to end this bloody war as soon as possible, and
any signs of real work raise our spirits no end. As a mere sideline
on the subject of politics in the army—two points of view have
been expressed by the C.O. and Squadron Leader. The C.O. said
the old army method of the horse trough was still the best way of
teaching a man patriotism. The S.L. said that we were all paid
certain rates for certain jobs by the Government and if we did not
do our work properly we were not keeping the contract. It is
extremely lucky that the bulk of the men here are, on their own,
anti-fascist, and feel this to be the purpose of the fight, otherwise
there would be no idealism to spur on fighting morale. It is very
difficult to write a decent letter as we are cut off from all civilization
(except an occasional newspaper) and surrounded by the monoto-
nous routine of peace-time soldiering. But we must keep our chins

* A batman is an English officer's orderly.—*Ed.*

16

up and do all in our power to win more and more people for the war and against defeatism.

This morning we had the first meeting of the debating society committee which I am on. Our first debate is for next Thursday. The subject is "Woman's Place Is in the Home." I proposed this subject as it appeals to the men; they all have ideas on it, and it will lead to some pretty good discussion when they get back to their tents. Among other subjects I put up were, "Tradition is a Hindrance to Progress" and "We Should Treat the Indians As Equals." . . .

You have little idea how badly we need the news of the second front—it is the difference between a body of good, stolid-humored Britishers and an inspired army of warriors. Our troop leader has just given us a talk—a sort of self introduction—which included an impassioned 20 minutes against the second front (of course, there are no politics in the army). Incidentally, I have yet to meet a junior officer who wants the second front. Today I had a driving test—or rather before the test I told the officer I knew nothing but *very badly wanted to know it* so I have been recommended for a *long* D. and M. course which will bring me up to the standard of a Driver-Mechanic—I hope to goodness it comes off as this will make me a *real* Armored Corps man and not a lopsided one.

This morning we went out on a scheme on foot in units representing tanks. We covered ten or more miles over ploughed fields, etc. It was magnificent exercise and although I felt pretty tired I enjoyed it no end. That sort of thing will make real soldiers of us.

But tonight I have had a terrible set-back. On parade this morning we were asked who had seen active service. I said I had. When we came back from the scheme I was informed that I was to go to an inspection by the Duke of Gloucester in a few days' time. This is apparently the purpose of asking about active service. This parade is a purely bull-shit parade. It will take several days to polish boots, brasses, etc. It will take days and nights for some eight Indian tailors to alter, clean, press, etc., etc.,

17

clothes for the white sahibs to wear like bloody waxworks. The Indians will, of course, not be on parade, the lucky fools. I have often been asked, "Have we got a fifth column here?" Yes, we have! For nothing could help the enemy more by undermining morale, destroying enthusiasm and making us incompetent fighters than this kind of tomfoolery.

. . . The above farce develops. This morning we had an inspection. The Duke's show is in five days' time. We are not to wear our inspection clothes for the next four days. On *the* day we get up at 5 a.m. Our clothes will be packed in boxes and taken by lorry to the scene of battle where we will get into them, etc. Sevastopol is falling and our C.O. is disappointed at the lack of polish on the topee chin straps.

July 3, 1942. Gulunche, Nr. Poona

Well, the Duke's show is over, at immense expenditure of precious petrol, wear and tear of vehicles, deadening bull-shit. The inspection was over in no time. The Duke merely shook hands with unit commanders and squadron leaders—the men just didn't exist. There were no bands, no music. No show could have been put on better calculated to emphasize the complete lack of interest our rulers have in getting the war over.

Today a General paid us a visit, and a fellow has just been brought into the guard room bringing some news of it. In one squadron they had many men in P.T. kit, some ready to box, some to do P.T., two basketball teams, etc., etc. These men were kept sitting about doing nothing for ages until a scout saw the General's car. The scout signaled, and immediately everyone began boxing, playing, etc. As soon as the General disappeared the men were marched back to their tents. This is how things are going on here. There are hundreds of men here compelled to do such bloody ridiculous things. . . .

As a result of the rain the country has a lovely rich earth and green look about it; what enormous wealth could be produced if real irrigation was organized!

I am feeling very tired and depressed, mainly because everything here is like a mad-house—apparently quite sane, however, to the superior inmates.

18

While on guard tonight I was thinking of Battersea and wrote this poem:
>When the edge of day's flag is tattered
>Long before hours terminate day's end
>In bitter wind,
>And birds' wings lag,
>And smoke crawls softly from the power-station chimney.
>
>When at the end of a long day's labor
>Night scrapes the clodded blade of day
>Metallic clean, and engines tire,
>Before this fire sleeps,
>Thoughts of you drift from the still smouldering embers.

July 28, 1942. Gulunche, Nr. Poona

I have just got back from 48 hours' leave in Poona. I bought five books all on science and one on religion in the "Thinkers' Library." I could get nothing on India at all. I had two excellent meals in a Chinese restaurant. I tried to see an Indian film (the Hollywood muck makes me feel sick) but was not allowed inside an Indian cinema. After getting the books and meals I went early to bed at the Y.M.C.A. This morning I had another good meal, a walk down the only street allowed to British troops (!)—we are prisoners all right out here, but more on this—and caught an early train back feeling much refreshed mentally and physically.

The reception for British troops out here is an insult. I am not referring to that given us by the Indians, but by our so-called countrymen. A soldier walks in Poona past large houses with well groomed gardens belonging to British officers, etc. He cannot get a room in the many big hotels—they won't entertain having him in. He is compelled to go to the Y.M.C.A. where there are no hot baths, no separate rooms, in fact, a bare barrack less comfortable than in our tents. Lady Lumley has given her name to a *typical canteen for the troops* where some white women do the serving "to show how patriotic we really are." It stinks!!

August 12, 1942. Gulunche, Nr. Poona

By the time you get this letter the arrest of the Congress

19

leadership* will be stale news. You will be well aware of the elementary fact that these arrests do nothing to solve the basic problem (namely, *the Indians' fight for their own freedom*)—except that it will teach the Indians to hate us all the more! Two sides are now emerging—one, positive, for an agreement on Pakistan** by Congress (this is the Communist Party's line—more on the C.P. in a minute); two, negative, a looking towards Japan for help (a line already adopted by Chandra Bose,*** and, from what one can hear, as well as inferences made by Gandhi, considered by sections of the peasantry—this fact was brought out strongly at the recent Students' Conference in Delhi).

Now about the Indian Communist Party—it is obvious to anyone who knows anything that (1) the C.P. was made legal as a final effort to disrupt Congress as it is the only party with any following among the people; (2) that as in Burma it has been made legal too late to prevent the Wardha resolution and propaganda. Now the position is that the Indian Communist Party stands for alliance with the British Sahib, but also is working for Indian unity, Pakistan, an Indian National Government *now*. Which raises a new problem for the British Raj—shall we suppress the C.P.I. again, or shall we have democracy in India as we have in Blighty and suppress their newspapers only?

This is all in the field of general politics. Among the fellows there is extraordinary confusion, especially brought out over the Congress business. Discussions go on night and day with views expressed ranging from two extremes: (a) I came to fight the Japs not the Indians, to (b) It would be all right to have a go at Gandhi and his Hindus; we should get some practice like the Japs

---

* On August 7, 1942, the Congress working committee had issued a resolution (an amended version of the Wardha resolution) restating its demand for the withdrawal of British power "so as to enable India effectively to become an ally of the United Nations and fight the aggressors." If this appeal was ignored, Congress would resort to a campaign of mass struggle on non-violent lines. The All-India Congress Committee endorsed this resolution on August 8, and requested Gandhi to open negotiations with the Viceroy for a settlement. But the next day, before Gandhi had the opportunity of opening negotiations, the Congress leadership (including Gandhi and Nehru) were arrested, following which riots broke out spontaneously.—*Ed.*

** A self-governing Moslem state, whose creation is proposed as part of a plan to divide India into two parts.—*Ed.*

*** Indian agent of Japanese imperialism.—*Ed.*

got in China. One has to keep one's head screwed on very tight, keep one's ear to the ground, and one's arguments apt.

August 20, 1942. Gulunche, Nr. Poona

As it is Saturday afternoon, I have retired to the canteen to read and write quietly. I must confess there is an ulterior motif for this exclusiveness. Parties from our squadron have been detailed and left camp to maintain law and order in a nearby town. This sort of warfare is so distasteful to me that I take every care not to be detailed.

The whole business is *tragic* to say the least. The Indians want independence, so as to fight for their independence against Japan. The white sahib says, No—not just verbally, but in numerous practical ways—no home guard, no mass people's army, no nuclei of guerrillas, no arrests and shooting of profiteers, a heavy hand on most urgently necessary development of Indian industry (as, for example, the careful suppression of the report of the American Industrial Mission) and last but not least, the continued arrogance, extravagance and domination of the white Raj.

Congress takes up the demand of the masses—good! Then Gandhi imposes pacifism, which means, in fact, sabotage of the struggle. But today things have gone so far that pacifism is impossible—so in place of a positive struggle, the people's movement takes an anarchist turn *in every way ideologically helped by the firm hand of authority*—i.e., arrest the leadership, give no concessions, call out the police and then troops.

No set of actions could be better suited to embitter *even more deeply* Anglo-Indian relations. For example, the ex-premier of Madras, Mr. Rajagopalachari, recently revolted against Nehru and Gandhi by proposing, and actively organizing a campaign on behalf of the recognition of Pakistan by Congress to get Hindu-Moslem unity. He was expelled from Congress. Now, after locking up the Congress leadership, the British have turned to Rajaji with honeyed words, only to be met with blunt condemnation for their exhibition of the firm hand.

One cannot foretell what will happen. The movement so far is confined to the towns, mainly angry demonstrations against police stations with a little shop breaking, telephone wire cutting, shop

21

closing, etc.; a small strike movement. As far as one can tell, the peasantry is not involved and the class-conscious proletariat is following the C.P.I. The movement is mostly among the students, shopkeepers and near-peasant town dwellers. As a purely personal comment it seems curious to find oneself on the side of the Cossacks —rather revolting in fact. Even though one does not agree with what the people are doing, one understands why they do it.

I have just seen the evening paper. Rajaji has written an article against the arson, etc., which is going on, and he is, of course, quite right, but this does not mean he has forgotten the real perpetrators of the trouble. Let us hope the present disorders stop soon and the masses consider the position once again *positively,* although it is a little difficult to see how this will happen when the one really great Indian Nationalist Party is suppressed and its leaders jailed.

I had a long chat with a friend of mine from another squadron who tells me the men there are worried about the situation. I see that the Labor leaders have called upon the Congress leaders to call off civil disobedience—how *brilliant!!* Doesn't the labor Party know that the Congress leaders are in jail, and that is why the rioting is going on, anarchistic because without leadership.

One of the men in my tent has just come back off leave. He had an eventful train journey with the Congress supporters. He is one of these objective liberals—educated, middle class. His conclusions are: (1) that these Indians in the main are kicking up a row for Gandhi's release and that the present campaign is *not* re the "Quit India" resolution; (2) that the presence of the British is synonymous with their low incomes, and therefore Indian independence has an economic foundation in the minds of the people; (3) and, by far the most serious of all, it is perfectly clear that Nazi and Jap propaganda is getting a wide hearing. This fellow is convinced that, from the reactions of his listeners to his own stories of himself and other lads from Blighty, etc., the propaganda of the British is futile or even nil.

One of the things I have already commented upon in my letters is that we are like prisoners out here; like lepers who are forbidden to enter the villages or Indian regimental quarters or in any way get to know the Indian people. Let alone the fact that we haven't

22

even thought of helping the villagers to organize a people's or guerrilla army.

The view from here is very lovely just now. A wide plain horizoned by blue, light-blue mountains. And in the foreground a group of laborers are scraping up the dry soil to sieve it for making cement paving. The women in all kinds of reds, deep purple, and pink, with shallow bowls which, when filled, they lift up on to their heads. The men in spotless white. The earth where they work is a light red, but a little distance back the landscape is a patchwork of very flat strips of black earth and rich green crops with dark green round trees dotted about.

Today has brought in the great news of the landing at Dieppe. Dare we hope that this is the beginning of the second front? Everyone is very excited and discussing this great news from every aspect. Tonight on orders I am detailed for an escort duty to a place some hundreds of miles from here. It will take several days so I should see a lot of India—only I'm afraid as a spectator and a very ignorant one at that, but I shall use my eyes.

August 27, 1942. Gulunche, Nr. Poona

The really important thing that has hapéned is the Dieppe raid, and the tremendous impetus it has given to the idea of opening a second front. Many of the men thought it was the second front and instead of being what we are, we went about as though life had a purpose and a future. Now that the show is over we have returned to normal. We read the news about the Red Army. Occasionally an odd man says, "Well, they'll attack soon, the winter is coming," but the overwhelming majority look hungrily for that news of the second front which Dieppe has proved to them as thoroughly practicable.

Tonight we had a joint debate between us and another squadron on should doctors be allowed to practice mercy killing. Not on the face of it a very interesting subject, but it was interesting to notice a number of the speakers showing that they are stepping out of their little individual selves and becoming social minded. An officer came up to me after the debate to inform me he had seen me speaking in Finsbury Square. A bit of a shock, what! But I am pleased, as we had a good talk afterwards.

It is only two days now before I am due to go on leave to Bombay. I hope to goodness I am able to go—I want so badly to get some books. I wrote to you recently that soon the question of the continued legality of the Indian C.P. would come up. Two or three days ago it was discussed by the *Times of India*. Things out here are extraordinarily interesting.

One thing I have learnt out here more than anything else is that life in England, and therefore one's outlook towards people and the world, is hopelessly divorced from the rest of humanity. When this war is over we must go to China, come back to India as civilian friends. This all sounds rather unpractical I know, and it probably is, but it just lets you know that my stay abroad this time is not having the effect of making me want to settle down at home after the war, but to see and learn more, much, much more.

The Sergeant Major assures me I shall get my leave. So I am very excited. Unless something happens, I shall be away on Monday.

August 30-September 7, 1942. On leave in Bombay

Here I am in the St. John's Institute in *Bombay*. I arrived after dark so I have not seen anything yet, except that from the gari which took me from the station to here, I saw some huge bookshops. I shall try during the coming days to get to know some Indian students. I am here entirely on my own—to tell you the truth I am glad as I shall not have to make army small talk or do things I don't want to do. . . .

My first day in Bombay has been a great success. I have bought a number of excellent books, "The Communal Triangle in India," by Mehta and Patwardhan. It is written in the tradition of Dutt's classic and if published at home, you should get it. All the other books are on man's early history.

Apart from book buying, I spent an hour or so in the Prince of Wales Museum—a pathetic effort for a nation with such magnificent sculpture as India, with such prehistoric cities as Mohenjo Daro of 3,000 B.C., whose baths, drainage, planning, etc., would do credit to any Indian city today. But even more important, from my point of view, it shows that what we are pleased to call civilization (i.e., sanitation, architecture, social organization

24

in townships, sculpture) are far older than has been the common opinion based on the sole example of ancient Egypt—the easiest to get at and the best preserved and therefore the most explored ancient society.

From the balcony outside my room I look out on the bay and can hear the waves breaking on the rocks. Wherever I have met Chinese people in India I cannot help contrasting, just from their appearance, the intense national pride of that great people with the still unformed nationalism of the Indian. The Indians have some way to go, but I wish we were here to help them instead of to play the Jap. . . .

Having got out I went for a long walk, very long, and was just about to turn back when I ran into some *friends*. And what a long talk we had together. It was marvelous. Tomorrow, and it seems for the rest of my stay in Bombay, I am meeting them, so my leave has turned out a real success. When they heard I was stationed at Poona, they gave me the name of someone who lives there. I am very excited at this because it may enable me to have a guide to see some of the great historic remains in the Poona district, a thing which I have been longing to do since I came to this country. In the bookshop I picked up a book on Indian sculpture which really is magnificent—it is of interest to know that in the making of New Delhi, Indian architects were not called upon, only Indian cheap labor.

I felt a new man tonight after meeting some friends to talk with. By the way, the legalizing of the Indian C.P. is progressing well. There are only 900 members still in jail, including the recognized leader of the Bombay working class. This, with Congress leaders in jail, shooting, whipping, rigorous imprisonment, profiteering and the black market should teach these wogs* the meaning of democracy—what?

This evening I have been out to an Indian meal in an Indian's house. On the way, my tram passed the body of a man, killed by a car or something, lying out in the road with people going by as though it were a dead cat or dog. India is bound to explode soon, and what an explosion it will be when it comes.

* An imperialist term of contempt for Indian natives.—*Ed*.

Yesterday evening I was invited out to the house of a friend, where I had the chance of meeting a number of Congress supporters and explaining to them the need for developing different methods of struggle, as the present methods were, in fact, helping the Japanese and helping the British Government carry through its provocation—started by the arrest of the Congress leadership—the purpose of which is to smash the organized nationalist movement here under the plea of smashing the fifth column!

Last night I had a very pleasant surprise. A leading comrade called in at the house—he was very pleased to see me. He is just out of doing two and a half years in prison—really isolation, as he told me the treatment was quite good—i.e., political prisoners and not à la criminal prisoners. He is president of the Bombay T.U.C. I am meeting him today and he is going to explain to me the position among the workers.

It is now more clear than ever that the arrest of the Congress leaders at the precise moment when it took place was an act of flagrant provocation on the part of the bureaucracy. It, of course, resulted in a wave of anger throughout the country and gave the British raj the long-sought opportunity to smash the nationalist movement—the organized nationalist movement. Certain elements in India (including Tata*) are egging on the Congressmen in their actions, which are precisely those which an unarmed people takes against an armed army of occupation (the Tata works is on strike; rail, telephone, wire, stations and looting sabotage). There is no doubt at all that some of this is directly led by Jap agents, and the Jap wireless (with Bose from Berlin) is giving *precise* instructions to the angry Congressmen.

The plan of the bureaucracy has already gone wrong because (a) they never expected such a mass (including Moslem) sympathy for and demand for the release of the Congress leaders—*all* sections are demanding this, (b) the resignation of Sir C. P. Ramaswamy Iyer as gesture that he who had taken a lead against Congress *could not form an anti-Congress government.* The bureaucracy now hopes to form what they are pleased to call an Indian National

* Tata Iron and Steel Co., Ltd.—*Ed.*

26

Government out of all recognized parties (the Congress will not be there as it is banned). But it is crystal clear that the whole country, including the rank and file Moslems, is just not interested in such a "National Government." A new storm is brewing with as much anger in its heart, with more clarity in its head as to aims and methods, and with less instinctive passion. The question is, will it come in time to save India from the Burma strategy of the British?

All Christians are working overtime today having a day of prayer. (Those Godless Russians don't realize the value of religion, and therefore in their crude Marxist materialist manner *will* spend the day killing Nazis!)

I have said a lot about going to bookshops, but I have never mentioned something which hits you in the face about the general trend of literature. 1. Hitler's *Mein Kampf* is on sale prominently at *every* bookstall—of course, proceeds go to the Red Cross. 2. Sex literature—from Van der Velde to the "confessions of a young wife"—is plastered all over every bookstall as well as large bookshops. 3. Bourgeois novels. 4. The "left" literature consisting of the usual vicious anti-Soviet explanations of the Soviet Union and Communism, plus a thin dribble of Pat Sloan's *Russia Without Illusions* and *Russia Resists*. Not only is Dutt's book on India banned, but so also is the Penguin book *Problem of India,* by Shelvankar. 5. There is a mass of religious-fanatical literature. Such is the state of affairs. Can you wonder that with their hatred of the British, some of the Indians, with their brains starved of anything practical, give way to rioting and listening to the practical voice from Tokio and Berlin coming over the ether?

Although the C.P. is legal, its meetings are banned if they wish to speak on Indian Affairs.

I see now the *New Statesman* is proposing a Government of Hindus and Moslems, who will be willing to function, while leaving the Army Command, etc., etc., in the hands of the British —*but that is no good*. It is precisely on this rock that the tide has burst. Indians have absolutely no confidence either in the British Burma strategy, nor have they any confidence in British promises, nor do they have the slightest desire to fight *under* British command and *under* British control. This is how the matter stands with the

27

mass of the Indians—and they are *the only people* who can beat Japan. Their demand is—let India fight under an Indian National Government as free allies of the British. *Nothing less* will induce the Indian masses to change their 150 years' accumulated hatred of the white sahib.

So far as T.'s ideas on India are concerned—he always used to argue that he had been here and I hadn't—I can only say he must have got himself mixed up with certain caste of high-class women and worn a veil—and a thick one—over his eyes permanently. I can think of no other logical explanation. One cannot look at life *incessantly* for 30 years through the golden lustre of a glass of whiskey—unless one is an absolute drink addict, and I know that T. was definitely not that.

. . . I have been for a lovely walk along the sea front and then took a tram to the Museum and went through the National History Galleries—really well laid out. The Museum was packed with Indians, who were all talking in the most excited way about the exhibits as though they enjoyed looking and seeing what they saw —I was reminded very forcibly of visiting museums in Moscow.

. . . This morning I heard a sound I haven't heard for a long time—an air raid siren. Which reminds me, I had a long talk with our friends about tasks arising out of air raids and mentioned the work around refugee centres. They have five of these in the whole of Bombay! So I urged that every step possible should be taken to get more, and described in as much detail as possible the reasons for this.

One of the things which, ever since I came to India, has been a source of wonderment and intense joy are the little Indian girls. There were some going round the Museum with all the solemnity of grown-ups—but they could not have been more than three years old and about 1½ ft. high. Their faces are very round, with very round dark eyes, and the hair is done flat to emphasize the round-ness. Sometimes the hair is cut like a European child's, but there is always such incredible dignity and poise.

There is an interesting example of how "we" are dealing with the Indian Problem. At Baramatti, Poona, there was some rioting about 2-3 weeks ago, with burning of a railway station, cutting telephone wires and attacks on police. A score or so were arrested

28

and given heavy sentences. There was then quiet. Now it is announced that a collective fine of 30,000 rupees has been imposed (excluding the police, authorities and scheduled classes!!). This is a classic example of how the bureaucracy *is creating hatred among the whole population*. In this atmosphere we shall probably be called upon to fight the Japs. Promising, isn't it?

And are we hated out here by the people? *Oh, no!* I say in all seriousness, God help us if the Japs come, unless the Government makes some move to repair the damage. This theme drums in my mind like a persistent warning. It is so elementary, so absolutely necessary. It is the, and the one and only, precondition for winning the war against the Japs. You people at home *must* stir up Blighty on this question. We English fellows came out here to fight the Japs and face the possibility of finding a grave in India. But we did not come out here as a suicide squad to be stabbed in the back by the British bureaucracy in Delhi and Whitehall. We did not come here to be killed by Indians provoked by the insane reactionary policy of Amery* and Co.

This morning I paid a visit to the Zoo. It looks just like the rest of this country. Exactly the same kind of parrot in the cage as out. Exactly the same pigeon in as out. The whole thing a mockery of a country extraordinarily rich in fauna.

From time to time some small-minded idiots have said to me— when you have got socialism, how will people occupy their time? Well, from just this few months' glimpse I've had of India (and then keeping in mind China, Siberia, Africa and Brazil), my suggestion would be to *discover the world we live on*. As yet we have only named vast areas on the map—some few, very, very few, have traveled over them—a few large firms have organized the exploitation of the human labor to be found there ready-to-hand. But the history of these places—thousands of years deep, upon which the present rests—is only scraped at with a prehistoric concept of history, as the Indian peasant "ploughs" his land. Our first duty lies with our own country, but when that is firmly set on its way, I know I shall want to come back to India, where I can feel I am with humanity and not just one of a stuck-up little part of it.

* Secretary of State for India until July, 1945.—*Ed.*

29

The civilized white sahib most certainly has jerked humanity out
of its antiquity. But now humanity will teach him to be human
once again instead of an arrogant beast.

I can hear the sea-waves breaking on the shore,
   I can hear the buses passing down the street,
I think the human voices ask "How long before,
   How many waves and buses pass before we meet?"

My candle burns the wick of time low down,
   While in night-silence, history turns the pages.
Wars and religion, imperial Gods are gone.
   The pavement where they trod winds through the ages.

My doors are shut. Yet in the world outside
   Humanity in birth-pangs gets no sleep.
The sea prepares to swell a further tide,
   Life hesitates before the final leap

To end all strife by elemental force.
   Even the slightest touch will leave its mark.
In endless stream the traffic flows its course,
   And bit by bit recedes into the dark.

September, 1942. On leave in Bombay
I had a very interesting time yesterday evening. I was taken round
to meet the wife of an Indian cotton mill owner. Things here get
more and more wonderful as one gets to know more. I now learn
that Indian industrialists are wanting to put up aircraft factories,
but the British won't let them. At this house I saw one of the
loveliest Indian carvings of two dancing figures—part of a wooden
frieze from a temple in South India.

The Bombay Council has rejected a resolution proposing to set
up two birth control clinics in Bombay on the grounds that such
advice "to wives whose health will not permit them to bear more
children, to husband or wife who is suffering from venereal
disease and to couples who wish to regulate the birth of children"
will mean an extension of prostitution and a lowering of morals.
The bloody hypocrisy of it—two doctors and of course the only
Christian voting against the resolution.

30

Last night I met a number of Indian students, C.P.I., and we had a splendid time. I gave them a report on what is happening, or rather *has* happened, in England since the war started. And then we had questions. It was a strange gathering. Everyone sat down on the floor. I did, too, until my knees began to ache, so they got me a box to sit on. Think of it—a white-sahib soldier in uniform sitting among wogs discussing politics as friends and equals! And not far away, outside, other white-sahib soldiers were patrolling the streets with tommy-guns, increasing the hatred of the Indian peoples *for them* just when the Japanese may invade.

All day today I have spent at the house of a friend, who has a marvelous collection of books on Indian and European Art. So I had one last revel in culture before going back to the regiment.

September 12, 1942. Gulunche, Nr. Poona

My leave is now over. I must tell you how it ended: I travelled by a midnight train, 3rd class, in a carriage packed with peasants and poor workers. A very interesting journey. Some Indian soldiers and one British were also there. I got the British one out of the way, asleep on the luggage rack. Then I dealt with the peasant question—how to get everyone, especially the women and children, a seat. The Indian soldiers behaved like Cossacks of old. They lay down on the seats, while women and children squatted on the floor and men stood. So I did the white-Sahib stuff—inverted—and made them get up and make room for the other people. This caused a stir—and just one more concrete piece of help in overcoming the present Congress line. A fitting end to a magnificent leave.

During the last two days since I have been back it has got much hotter, as though before a storm, and I have felt off-color with a perpetual headache. I am continually struck by the appalling contrast here and on leave. I am back again now with racial ˙hatred, anti-nigger sahibs, etc., which is depressing, however scientific one may be about it. There is one thing, many of the old sweats are being sent back to their original regiment, so they are happy again.

We are to go out on a lot of schemes. I cannot say more about them than that the fellows complain bitterly of the unnecessary destruction of crops that takes place. The interesting point is that

31

many of the men are closely related to small farmers, or are such themselves, and feel very acutely about these acts of vandalism which, in their opinion, could be avoided. In their minds this is creating a sympathy for the Indian peasant. But what is it doing in the minds of the Indian peasant other than making another cause of hatred for their over-lords? The question of compensation for war damage of this kind and confiscation of property for war purposes has been a bone of contention raised often by Congress.

Of course any discussion on this topic invariably brings out the old soldier. ("It serves the bastards right; they are a defeated nation and should stay like it; they're black outside and yellow in. I've seen them in riots," says the white sahib who was armed with armored car, machine-guns, rifles, horse, revolvers, etc.) And no argument will change these idiots—although one should be clear that these men are often very decent as individuals, and this "wog" insanity is the release mechanism for years of being ordered about, spied upon, fooled, and what is called disciplined or "broken in." But we who do see sense, in addition to much patient explaining, need the help of history, and especially of the Indians themselves. The Chinese are greatly esteemed, not as a result of the arguments of some who faced facts, but by their own actions *in addition*.

The only development now taking place, alongside continued disorders on a decreased scale, is definitely an increased demand for unity and for an Indian National Government. Churchill's speech* on India was just filth. It may have fooled some people in Britain and America, as well as the flunkeys out here, but as regards the vast mass of the Indian people (as well as the Jap and Berlin radios, worse luck) they dismiss the speech with the remark: "He hasn't even taken the trouble to think out some new argument, to invent some new 'facts.'" The situation here is developing according to its own logic.

September 19, 1942. Gulunche, Nr. Poona
I have today made another effort to get some D. & M. training. Let us hope with some result. I also had a row from our S.S.M., whose mentality is that of a beaten child and whose concept of war

* September 10, 1942. In the speech Churchill implied that the riots were a deliberate plan of Congress in order to help the Japanese.—*Ed.*

is approximately that of a mounted guardsman outside St. James' Palace. He will make quite a good soldier when he has been in action against a modern army for about four hours. This should make a man of him and lay the basis for him to learn from his fellow human beings what the war is about. He is an intelligent bloke, but a typical product of the peace-time army, especially the British army in India. Of course the above remarks apply to most of the regular soldiers, who are sergeants, etc.

The above business came up today when we were put on revolver. We drew the revolvers—each one signed for. Then who to take the class? I was forbidden to do so by the S.S.M., so I couldn't—*i.e.,* wasn't allowed to—so as no one else could, we returned the revolvers and did nothing. The sergeant in charge knows perfectly well I am well capable of instructing at this arm. But no! His attitude is: "The S.S.M. says Corporal Branson musn't do the job; there's no one else who can, so —— him, we won't do the revolver." You see the mentality that rules the camp? —— the S.S.M. or —— the C.O., but *never* "we must learn what we can, as best we can now, so as to beat the Japs." It is hell, especially as one knows that soon, possibly very soon, we may be in action. And in a modern tank there is so very much one wants to know, *absolutely instinctively,* in order to think tactically as quick as possible.

I have in my tent one of those intellectuals—lower middle-class school teacher—who is of the really infuriating type. We have just had an argument about the Red Navy. And believe it or not, his two points were these: "Russia is a land power, and therefore has a large army," and "Russia has a rotten navy because look at what happened to it against the Japanese." These arguments are made with all the authority of an H. G. Wells. What can one do to a brain so hopelessly unconnected with reality—and he teaches the young!

We are all feeling pleased tonight. At midnight we leave for a two days' outing. The place we are going to is a lake. There is one thing I love doing, and that is being out in the open, sleeping in the open, and so on. I will finish this letter when I come back. . . .

We left camp at 1:30 a.m. and started off towards Nira. Here I

33

got a really exciting surprise. As we entered the village everything was dead still. We were driving without lights. But the sky was clear, with almost a full moon. When we came half way down the only street I saw a great crowd of peasants, men with their white turbans and white linen cloth round them, sitting by the roadside. And among them sat many women in brilliant colors, lit up by the moon. With no stage and only a back-cloth with painted scenery, two men, lit by ordinary hurricane lamps, were acting a play to a large audience.

That is all I saw as our lorry went past. But what ideas crowded through my brain as we went on through the night. Of Indian student youth going to the peasants of Bengal, showing them in plays how to unite against Japanese Fascism. All that I have so often read about became perfectly practical. How I wanted to stay, to see the play through, and talk to the peasants about it! But our worlds are different, so I had to go on with the white sahibs in lorries.

As we drove through the villages we passed many carts with their lamps hung below on the axle, moving at the pace of a sleepy bullock. On their outskirts, tiny shelters, not more than 3 feet high and 7 feet long, clustered, where the poor—in this country where millions are poor these just exist—wait through their life-time. Such clusters of rags, tins, old mats, etc., are to be seen in every village and town. Millions of human beings must live in them. Oh, why am I here as a soldier and conqueror, and therefore the prisoner of my conquest?

I cannot stress too much the appalling mass poverty, dirt, ignorance and backwardness of the people. Yet *we* travelled in modern lorries, went across railway lines and at times passed a factory with machinery. Past miles and miles of tilled soil, with not a sign of a tractor—only a bullock, with a single blade scraping the earth. Past village after village where human beings live in hovels; a bit of a roof resting against an old stone wall, with mud floor; a shelter of matting laid over sticks, improved with bits of tin, old carpet, some tenting, perhaps; just high enough for the occupants to sit up in on their haunches.

This type of dwelling is the same as that used by man 50,000 years ago. At Mohenjo Daro, on the Indus, a town of 3,500 B.C. has been unearthed. There were remains of carts exactly the same as now used by the peasants in Sind. And so on.

But these peasants are not unobservant. Every time an aeroplane flies overhead, a lorry goes through the village, a nail is hammered in the coffin of feudalism, and from the soil of ancient India springs yet one more Indian nationalist. A journey through this country is indeed painful—there is such a vast mass of human happiness, human intelligence, gone to waste.

September 26, 1942. Gulunche, Nr. Poona

It says in the *Times of India* today that about 5,000 signatures have been taken in Ahmedabad by the local Communist Party to a memorandum which has been forwarded to Rajagopalachari and Jinnah* stressing the urgency of a rapprochement between the Congress and the Moslem League as a preliminary to the establishment of a National Government led by Nehru and Jinnah. Over 100,000 signatures from about 700 villages of Kaira district are being sought to a memorandum to be forwarded to the Government demanding the establishment of a National Government and the release of Congress leaders.

There are continued acts of violent pro-Congress demonstrations —mainly among students. The proletariat and the peasantry are almost completely quiet. From all quarters the question of unity is being voiced. In the Council of State debate on the present situation, the main points of the C.P.I.'s line were voiced time and again. It is an extremely interesting set-up. Any Japanese invasion must be resisted by the British. The concrete impact of Japanese invasion and the resistance of the British to the Japs will, now that the Gandhi policy has been experienced for what it is and the C.P.I. has had time to give the correct line, concretize the latent tendencies among the proletariat and peasantry for independence and nationalism.

I have been in the gunnery wing all day where it seems I am on the permanent staff, which is something to keep my mind alive.

There is more news of the movement towards unity here. You can take it that this is the only real positive movement in hundreds

* The President of the Moslem League.—*Ed.*

35

of resolutions, petitions, discussions, speeches being sent to the Governor, Jinnah, Raja, Nehru, etc. The bombing, etc., is practically at an end. But there is one thing that is quite definite—the Indian masses are completely apathetic about *our* war effort. The British are loathed, and only an Indian National Government will make this India's war. Indians just don't believe one word of our claims to be fighting for freedom, etc. This is the truth of the set-up out here, and no other explanation is correct.

October 3, 1942. Gulunche, Nr. Poona

I am again on a 24-hour guard at Gulunche. With me is one of the old sweats. He started off by saying that he had heard of trouble at. . . . When asked what had happened, he replied dramatically, "Women raped." It would have made me laugh outright—fancy Congress students demonstrating for the release of Nehru by raping women—had it not been such excellent Fascist propaganda.

Some great mental analyst should make a study of the regular soldier in India. I took my book on Human Origins to the gunnery wing today to read during the break. A young regular, aged 23, with seven years' service, looked at the photos for a bit, read some sentences, and closed it, saying, "Those bastards write books like that to make millions out of poor soldiers." And no explanation on my part could convince him otherwise. It all emphasizes how deeply has the sense of oppression, humiliation, and lack of human friendliness or suspicion, been driven upon their minds by the imperial army machine. I am not in the least surprised nowadays after getting to know these fellows, why they're not interested in fighting in this war. *They don't believe in it.*

. . . It is now past 4 a.m. I have had a long read and made some notes. In front of me is a kerosene lamp. Dozens of moths, insects, beetles keep madly flying at it. After watching a bit, and thinking about the Red Army, I wrote this poem:

> Sleep on, sentries, through your turn of duty,
> The night is dark, stressed by the bugle moon,
> These insects warn you of the futility
> Of mistaking lights and flying out of turn.

36

Look how they beat against the glass!
With frenzied repetition they are stunned.
Yet had they made no flight to reach false stars
Death would have been a sleep with no wings singed.

Sleep on, sentries, while your beds are safe.
Your sanity commends you to long nights.
These brainless idiots emulate the brave
Who, in their madness, dare celestial flights

Without a hope of getting back alive.
Sleep on, you sentries, no need to wake up now.
Who was the fool is walking on your grave;
He met the new day rising while you slept, long ago.

The Sergeant slept all night and went without so much as a word of thanks. I find these nights on guard go very quickly if one can get into a good, useful book.

October 12, 1942. Dhond Camp, Poona

Please note change of camp. I am now quite alone in my barrack room. All the fellows are either at the cinema or Y.M.C.A. Next week there is to be an added "attraction" of a brothel under official patronage. I need make no comment on this.

A new order has been issued to the effect that we must salute Indian officers. This has produced a flow of indignant remarks from the regulars.

The dhobi-walla—or laundry man—has just brought our clean clothes. So out on the verandah is the shouting, bawling, threatening which invariably signifies that a white sahib is talking to a wog—showing him the true meaning of British *democracy.*

The other day I had a row with one of these white sahibs. He accused me of lowering the prestige of the whites because I am on friendly terms with the tea sellers, fruit sellers, etc. Especially am I friendly with the little boys—mere children—who earns annas in the camp getting cups of tea, etc. These kiddies get *no* education and see life in the raw. Anyway, I answered, much to the pleasure of other men just out here, that, of course, the well-known fact that white sahibs go into cheap brothels with native women must do much to uphold this prestige.

You have no idea how abysmal is the "cultured" life we are made to live. Never allowed to learn anything about India or the Indians. Never once have we been shown anything to do with the Indians. The other day I had an argument with an old sweat on India—the usual, "I've been here N years so I know." So I asked him if he'd ever met an Indian Trade Unionist or any Indian public figure when he went on leave instead of the usual girl in a brothel, the char (tea) walla, etc. He not only admitted no! but asked "What is a trade unionist?" And this man is a soldier for democracy.

This morning the idiot with whom I had the argument about "prestige" smacked a chicko (the one who fetches cups of tea) across the face. The little chap was being shouted at by this "gentleman" and didn't understand English. He was bewildered when struck and then burst into tears. But I soon comforted him and gave him an anna.

All day I've been in the gunnery wing on odd jobs. There are some Indians—men, women and little children—who come there to work. The children don't work but come with their parents. I've seen wee babies being taken by their parents to the work place. There they are put down on one side while the elders—over 10 years?—work. It is scandalous that there are no crèches or schools for these children. Anyway, I made friends with them by giving them fruit and nuts I bought from the fruit walla. Needless to say, my ignorant behavior always leads to an argument with those who know how to treat natives. Of course, there are those who say in a charitable way, "You'll change when you've been here longer." How well I remember the wise ones saying ten years ago, "You'll change when you grow older." But now see what *they're* saying about the Soviet Union. Why, only today a conversation between a sergeant and a one-pip officer [an officer of low rank] was overheard. To this effect:

O. What's the latest news about Stalingrad?

S. They're holding on. In fact, it seems they're beginning to push the Germans back. It's a marvellous show.

38

O. Yes, it certainly is. There must be something in this man Stalin.

And I know very well who is going to change in their attitude to the Indian people—it won't be me.

Last night I went to the cinema to see *One of Our Aircraft Is Missing*. Excellent; with an excellent result on the spirit of the men. The most serious gap in the training of the army is the complete absence of propaganda. But the remark by the Dutch woman about the Germans, "They are the most miserable people, they want so badly to be friends," hit the mark. It described so very vividly our position out here. We jack up our own "cheerfulness" among ourselves in order to hide our loneliness and our lack of friends out here.

October, 25, 1942. Dhond Camp, Poona

The latest developments in India concern Congress. Congress consists of (1) Bourgeois nationalists such as Gandhi; (2) People's nationalists such as Nehru, Azad, etc.; (3) Communists; (4) Congress Socialists; and (5) Forward Block and fifth column. Now the latest information gathered from the character of the police arrests is that although the acts of sabotage and incendiarism are without any doubt organized by the Forward Block and fifth column, the overwhelming majority of arrests are of honest Congressmen of categories 1, 2 and 3. The bureaucracy here is so excited about this God- (Berlin-Tokio) given opportunity to smash the nationalist movement, that they leave free the real disruptors. But I have not the slightest doubt that if the Japs attack India the British Government will be forced to release Nehru, etc., in order to defend India with any degree of success.

In the meantime the Indian C.P. is doing tremendous work to clear up the mess produced by "those who know best." Their line is everything for the unity of the people and the unity of the people comes first, for the defense of India, for Indian freedom. Anyway, the smashing of the Congress goes on, to be followed in a short time when it is complete, by the round-up of Congress socialists and Forward Block.

Now that the Congress organization has been smashed to pieces, dozens of nitwits, large and small, are all proposing their blue-

39

prints for future "settlements." Meanwhile the workers and peasants go on living, taking due note of events while they labor, and preparing for the next manifestation that a free India can fight, work and progress as well as China.

November 7, 1942 Dhond

This afternoon I went for a walk in Dhond City! A modern railway line with great steel engines runs by the straw, tin and sackcloth "houses" of the people. A huge engine of war roars past a settlement of the poorest of the poor. Dhond is derelict, filthy and poverty-stricken—I mean where the people live, not the workshops, etc. Whatever is put across the Indian people, nothing can argue against the logic of their living conditions in contrast to the motor cars that mock their bullock carts and them—for they, too, drive the motor. And, however much people at home believe in British imperialism, there are four hundred millions who *know* by bitter daily experience the reality. Of course, this is not exactly the ideal background for Indian support for the British war effort— but I have dealt with this very fully in previous letters. Only the sight of Dhond, the daily sight of men and women walking to work (cheap manual labor with a vengeance) in contrast to the lavish munificence of the gods of war constantly reminds one of the "Indian Tragedy."

But all this is not abstract. The other night I had a hell of a row over a young Indian being hit by a great white sahib and then being shouted at by the R.O.C. like a dog. I am certain I shall not end my tour of duty in the army in India without getting into some trouble through sticking up for the Indians. But I know who is right. . . .

I have just got back from a swim—it was lovely. It is of course piping hot—a cruel sun that makes the earth sand-dry even within a few yards of the water's edge; and the green, long leaves of the young sugar cane glint like bayonets. But oh, the ghastly poverty of the Indian people! Wherever one goes it is the same thing. Little clumps, sometimes village size, of broken stone walls, sacking, bits of tin, corrugated iron roofing propped against a wall, and matting, called "home" by millions of human beings. In the

40

middle, or nearby, a temple or a church, and far away in the cities
the swine who live wealthily.

There is little news. I am very fit, working hard and quite happy
under the circumstances.

November 14, 1942. Dhond

Just after I had posted my last letter to you a really exciting thing
happened. I ran across a friend who had lived in India all his
life. We had a long talk together. He lives near here, and so is
going to lend me good books from time to time. This bucked me
up no end. I also get a good paper regularly.

November 25, 1942. Dhond

In my last letter I spoke of a friend whom I had met. I met him
up by the Cinema, where he was in the habit of coming quite
openly on week-ends. This last week-end he didn't come on the
Sunday, but on Monday. He had on him some copies of *People's
War* (the C.P.I. weekly paper) and a book or two for me, as well
as an official receipt for a donation I had given him. While he was
talking to a fellow the Regimental Police came up and told him
to go with them to the Adjutant. He was then taken immediately
to a civil magistrate, who sentenced him to six months' rigorous
imprisonment, plus a fine of 50 rupees or alternative of another
three months. The charge was for being in a prohibited area!
Now, added to this, the stinking swine are spreading the story that
he was distributing Congress material under cover of being a
C.P.er. Such is the legality of the C.P.I.! Party members are being
and have been arrested all over India for being active against
Congress, but in reality because they fight for Indian Unity and
National Government. We felt very sad and angry about this
happening, but we have replied as best we can by a "Lenin enroll-
ment" campaign. God, how things reek out here! I have written
a lot about India in my letters, but don't think I exaggerate in the
slightest degree.

By the way, a slight injury to my hand was done under almost
symbolical circumstances. The Squadron Leader, an officer—both
holding an ankle—the Squadron Sergeant-Major and Sergeant
with the help of a large trooper were all together trying to get me

to do a hand-stand (*i.e.,* one hurls oneself until one arrives upside-down, supported on one's hands). While they were all engaged in this piece of essential war effort I was having a hearty laugh (with many other B.O.R.'s laughing also) and thinking to myself, "You stupid idiots, why don't *you* try to stand on your *feet*. I will be only too pleased to help you."

December 16, 1942. Dhond

There is now a famine on in the Bombay area. When we arrived here there was one on in the Orissa area. Of course the glib explanation is crop failure, rain failure, etc. But come and see the Indian peasantry! With wells from which a bullock team draws water in a skin trough. With a plough that scratches what one is pleased to call a furrow with one blade. The task of providing modern machinery (with houses, roads, railways, etc., etc.), is a job that would occupy British industry for generations.

Tonight I have written for a week's reservation for leave in Bombay—let's hope it comes off.

December 24, 1942. Dhond

Today is Christmas Eve. The atmosphere in India is now sober and it is more than likely that people are doing some very deep thinking, not so much about the future, but about the present, the present policy of Jinnah, the present leadership of Congress, and of course the *ever*-present white sahib (who doesn't need much real thinking about, anyway!).

An entertainment party, including a conjuror, has turned up to entertain us. It is sincerely hoped that the conjuror will do the Indian Rope Trick and the Adjutant will go up the rope.

I should be going on leave in a few days.

December 28, 1942-January 4, 1943. On leave in Bombay

Here I am in Bombay. I had originally intended staying at the St. John's Institute where I stayed last time. But this Christmas I've had as much as I can stand of drunken revelry and at the last minute I remembered my leave spread over New Year's Eve so I decided to go to a posh [swanky] hotel where I could get good food, good bed, hot baths and *quiet*.

42

My first day has been quite successful. I've bought two of Pat Sloan's *How the Soviet State Is Run*. I went around to the Party headquarters, had a long talk and got some pamphlets.

It is clear that now, on top of the anti-Congress campaign, a wide food shortage is looming up all over India. It has already affected the middle class as well as the workers and peasants. Food hoarding and black marketing is rampant. But the most serious aspect is that while this affects the workers and peasants very badly they will not tell the police, they will not co-operate with the authorities although they know the offenders *because of their hatred of the white sahib. . . .*

. . . This morning a friend of mine, in the regiment, called for me at 10 a.m. and we went to the Party Center where we were immediately welcomed to an Indian meal. We took our boots and socks off and sat on a little straw mat to eat an ordinary meal. It was really great. Afterwards we were shown the Lenin Room and talked with a number of comrades. They have lent us some copies of *Labour Monthly* and *World News and Views* which we are now reading. We then went for a walk around the book shops and bought up *every copy* of Sloan's book—we must get enough lit. for the next three months. While I was at the Party Center, one Indian rank and file comrade gave me a postcard picture of Joe. This lad had signed it on the back "With red greetings from . . . his name." Wasn't it sweet of him? I promised him I'd have it up in my tank if ever I went into action. I am going to leave a note for another friend to join us and go to a cinema this evening. . . .

. . . This morning the three of us went along to the Party Rooms where we spent quite a long time reading and talking. We then went to one of the big bookshops, just looking. We had lunch at a Chinese restaurant and then all departed to our own ways.

The black market here is on an enormous scale. In all the industrial towns in India there is a food shortage becoming serious; there have been already a few food riots, looting of shops—of course, this is just what the fifth column and bureaucracy want. The arresting of Party members is now taking place on quite a large scale, because the Party are demanding People's Food Committees, etc., and are doing propaganda in the food queues. In

Bombay the workers are in the queues for eight hours a day. The Government has far too few grain shops for emergency distribution and these only stay open for three hours. The arresting of Party comrades is according to pattern. When our comrades were out trying to stop rioting as a result of the arrest of Congress leaders the police arrested them. When our comrades are trying to explain, to keep order in the food queues and a riot starts, the police arrest them. Still, after months have passed since the Party was declared legal, many leading comrades are in prison.

But, not to digress, the food shortage affects even the middle class and yet you can go into the hotels and restaurants and buy what you like. In this hotel, breakfast, lunch and dinner are all five-course meals. In yesterday's evening paper it speaks of 10,000 bags of wheat being bought for Delhi and adds the comment, "and particular care is being taken to prevent the incoming wheat from disappearing underground" (N.B.!). Incidentally, there is, in the same paper, a three-column account of the growth of Bombay's underworld. All very good, but the article begins "Sheltering behind legal loopholes, and encouraged by police pre-occupation with more urgent (!) and important (!) tasks, etc."

Never have I felt so depressed; so incapable of doing anything to meet the huge situation; so little able to atone for the stinking, filthy, crooked, hypocritical bastards of so-called Englishmen who rule this great country. The only thing is to do everything one can in one's own little sphere, so that when the great Indian people rise for freedom they will find some white sahibs at least are civilized and angry. Especially must one understand India as a sector of the world war. The essential difference of this war to the last is the unequal development of the various fronts. But that does not mean the war has not come to India, it simply means that here the forces are not so in the open as on the Russian Front, not so conscious of themselves nor so clear cut.

. . . In tonight's paper there is an important article on the food situation in Bombay. The following points are made: (1) Food stocks in the city are not likely to last more than two months . . . the authorities have discussed food rationing and "it is likely the scheme will be enforced by the middle of *March next*." (2) The mills have curtailed supplies to their workers in order to cope

44

(N.B.) with the situation; the paper reports a strike of workers in one of the mills against this. (*Note*: You know that the factory workers as a whole remained firm during the days following the arrest of the Congress leaders—only because they were led by the Party. It was no secret at the time that many factory owners— pro-Japanese in their anti-British struggle—did everything, including lock-outs, invitations to Congress agitators, etc., to incite the workers. It all failed—*but* the food shortage *may* be their next weapon, and tonight's news looks as if it *is*.)

You know that Calcutta is being bombed. But do you know that an acute food crisis is raging throughout Bengal? In this rice-producing province there is practically no rice. There is a coal crisis in Calcutta. Food queues are everywhere and food riots are already reported. Such is the mass basis prepared by Linlithgow* and Co. for our armies to reconquer Burma!

The *Times of India* now has an important article on the food situation. It writes: "The people of Bombay will not be able to have any large supplies of wheat for some months unless Australia agrees to export. The present stock of rice, jowar and bajri in the city are expected to last for two months," and again, "Large crowds wait in rows in front of Government grain shops from early morning in order to get their daily requirements of food grains, and scores of people return disappointed owing to the depleted supplies and imperfect arrangements made in the shops."

Now the food situation has been getting steadily worse *for months* past, yet the Committee of the Grain Merchants' Association, Bombay, has wired to the Viceroy urging him "to impose an embargo on exports and re-exports of foodstuffs from India . . . since the outbreak of war, exports of foodstuffs in large quantities have been allowed and believes that if stringent measures to stop them are not taken promptly, serious unrest may take place." (Note, of course, what has finally moved the committee of the G.M.A. is not the hunger of the workers but their anger.)

I am now going out for my evening stroll—then some reading and to sleep. Tonight they see the New Year in and already the

---

* Lord Linlithgow, Viceroy of India before Wavell.—*Ed.*

streets are noisy with drunks—when are we going to open the second front?

. . . This evening's paper has this bit on the food situation. "The Government of Bombay have decided to freeze the stocks of bajri held by merchants in Bombay city. Orders are expected to be served on the merchants any moment. Under the order, the whole stock will be acquired by Government and will be sold at a fixed rate. The decision has been taken in view of the tremendous rise in price of bajri during the past fortnight. It is stated that owing to the absence of control over bajri, heavy purchases were made by speculators in bajri during the past two weeks with the result that the rate has now shot up from Rs. 80 per candy to Rs. 130." Of course, it remains to be seen which of the following will be done by the Government: (1) Shoot the speculators; (2) confiscate their holdings of bajri; or (3) pay them a fair price, i.e., Rs. 130. We shall see, but I can make a safe bet it won't be 1 or 2.

Anyway, don't worry! At a society wedding in Bombay on December 30th "several hundred friends and relations (of the married couple) drank their health with enthusiasm. Followed a sumptuous party at which the guests were entertained with a lavish hospitality that was extraordinary, even for such weddings. Some time later the guests sat down to dinner which had to be taken in relays." The wedding was attended by the daughters of the Governor of Bombay—some war effort.

This morning I went to the usual place. Read the latest copy of *People's War** and after much insisting got the comrades to give me some work to do. I checked over a number of typed copies of extracts from the "Colonial Question"—which, incidentally, I was very glad to read again. I then did some work on a translation one of them had made of a Soviet story. At five o'clock I went to see Mrs. Wadia, where I had tea and looked through a book of reproductions of Soviet paintings—very academic, but, thank God, of people doing things. Mrs. W. gave me a book by that egotistical ass, Charlotte Haldane, which I will try to read.

I have just been for my evening stroll. As usual I went into the

* Indian Communist Party's weekly newspaper.—*Ed.*

46

Coffee Club to have an iced coffee. In came one of our officers—
a second lieutenant. Looked at my shoulder tabs and sat down
at the same table. He has a fortnight's leave and has spent most
of it drunk and in low haunts, has a woman and a borrowed motor
car. I asked him if he knew India at all well. No, but he knows
Bombay, especially the haunts, better than his home town, Belfast.
"Back home one can never get away from one's parents—here
there is nobody to watch what you do or where you go." After
this very enlightened conversation, I left him.

I went to the Victoria station, passing on the way hundreds of
people sleeping on the pavement, to find out tomorrow's trains
to Poona.

I caught the train after saying goodbye to my friends. The
journey was quite uneventful. At Poona I stopped for a meal and
then back to camp. I am feeling a little sad as things out here
are so dreadful. The arrest of the Congress leaders does not abolish
the class struggle nor imperialism. I fear that we may again be
called out to maintain law and order—don't misunderstand me—
not to shoot the speculators, landlords, government officials, but to
deal with the angry people.

January 25, 1943. Dhond, Nr. Poona

I am in a predicament. Lots of really interesting things have
happened this week but I can't describe them as they are connected with military doings. I am very fit, doing a lot of reading
and having many good discussions about various things. Included
with this letter are a number of pages of notes on peasant life.
These notes were made in a very rough form some weeks ago
when I had the incredible luck to find some deserted farmsteads
and so could wander around them and inside them making notes.
When this war is over we must decide to spend some time, perhaps
a couple of years, living in a peasant country, among peasants.

I have mentioned several times that I am making notes for a
book on the history of art—it would be absurd to propose such
a history without an understanding of peasant art. This is not to
be got by merely reading books on the subject—but also by making
a serious effort to understand why a human being should not only
make a little pulley but should fashion it in a particular shape and

47

mark lines and patterns on it. Or, again, why, among people who are so intimate with cows, goats, trees, etc., should one find a complete absence of realism and a totally stylized art of sculpture and drawing. You can well understand how excited I was to go into these houses. Incidentally, while prying about I ran into a group of peasant men—herdsmen to be precise. They wanted to tell me about everything the moment I made it clear to them, by signs and queries, what I was doing.*

* The following is a selection from the author's notes. The accompanying illustrations are omitted.

There was a certain amount of brick decoration. The end walls of the farm house were of rough stone to about 6 ft. and for the remainder of flat red brick. The patterns of decoration were madt by (a) turning the brick to have one corner jutting out; (b) making a ledge to emphasize a line; and (c) sinking the brick about 1 in. behind the general wall surface.

In one house, stuck into the plaster around a door, broken glass bangles were pressed to make a pattern. The broken pieces were all colors (glass, etc.). I found, in one room only, a similar use of broken bangles. Over one doorpost were stuck strips of brightly-colored paper. One stone wall made of squared stones had been colored black and white check according to the stones. The main entrance doorways, built round with small, flat brick had a great variety of pattern by protrusion and insertion of brick, coloring of bricks to make a pattern, coloring of mortar between bricks, etc.

A brief inspection of peasant farm houses suggested that house-building originated from the shelter provided by a cliff, a bank or a tree (edge of wood) *not* a cave. The place chosen being the site of water. Every farm has a well here. This develops to the building of walls of rough stone (dykers in Scotland—a trade now almost exinct there) and palisades or wicker mats. Only later do men build walls around them and for long these auxiliary walls are hinged on one main wall facing the prevalent wind, etc.

By the main building are set up sheds, either as a continuation of the main wall or independent. But the whole group spreads round the well.

The houses are built of rough stone, thin slab brick and plaster. This plaster is used sometimes as bricks, as mortar to hold stones or bricks, as inside lining to walls, etc.—it is a mixture of earth, clay and dung. The insides of the rooms appear to be washed down with a soft brush to make it quite smooth.

The stone craftsmanship is particularly noticeable in the construction of wells. Again all to one pattern. The wells are always dug *round,* never square. And down the side is a spiral of steps, large stone jutting out from the stone lines sides. In most there is no hand grip but in some a smaller stone projection is provided. A well may have just a single channel for the drawn water to flow or multiple with troughs to hold water for washing, etc. The most profound revolution in Indian peasant economy could be achieved by killing one out of every two bullocks and providing a petrol pump to the wells. It is no use killing the bullocks without providing alternative power to draw water. And, above all, the zeminders, landlords and bankers must not reap the benefit.

In a fair-sized village I found several clay models of bulls. One was painted white all over and then profusely covered with patterns in purple, green and gold. Another was left the color of clay but decorated with strips of red and gold paper stuck round the horns. These models, while still stylized, were extraordinarily lively.

48

February 1, 1943. On the move

My last letter had a number of notes on Indian peasant art. The B.B.C. has just announced the loss of a considerable amount of air mail, which probably means the notebook I sent on peasant art and a number of articles on India have been lost. I am very sorry about this.

Recently we have been on the move, and after a very busy week —and incidentally an extremely interesting and instructive one— we are once again at Nira Tank. This time the crops are golden ripe and, dotted all over the wide-stretching fields, are groups of peasants hand-gathering the seed. Whole families, men, women and little children are out all day. Some have built tents of straw and sticks; open air "kitchens." Wherever there are small children, they are put down at the foot of an enormous tall bundle of millet stalks—sometimes just tied near the top, sometimes wound round with a sari (peasant women wear pahrans—huge pieces of brightly-colored cloth—cotton). How very, very much I longed to paint and draw. . . .

An amusing incident happened on the journey here. In one town through which we passed, stuck up prominently in the main street was the old flag with hammer and sickle. It caused quite an amount of comment.

One of the officers with us has given me much food for thought. He is a stickler for machine-like organization. Now as this *never* happens in real life—as you and I learnt ages ago—he spends most of his time in a state of frantic worry and despair. The Spanish war taught me that war is even worse than normal life in this respect. A commander who expects his command to work like a machine is a bad modern soldier. The side which wins today is the side which can achieve a minimum of machine organization with a maximum of initiative.

The good news has just been told that we have another full day here. I shall enjoy this very much—it is very much colder here than on our previous visit—but it is so very beautiful.

February 6, 1943. On the move

Things here are going strong. The Communists, made legal by the British because they supported the war, still have many leaders in jail, their members are constantly being arrested, they are not allowed to hold public meetings or processions in most provinces. In Bengal, most threatened by the Japs, the repression is the worst.

This week we have been on the move camping and sleeping out. It is almost impossible to convey the vast richness of insect life in India. An insect so like a stick that it has the notches one finds in twigs—a large grasshopper with wings so like leaves as to have vein marks, etc. Then the red ant that covers the bole of a tree for many feet up with mud passages. One lot of these ants has a nest on a low branch—about the size of a football—covered with dead leaves on top—it is made with mud and straw (bricks!!) and the whole lower part has a surface of folds to resemble the curved surfaces of dried leaves. The other day I saw an *enormous* butterfly with red rear wings. The chief interest was in its flight. It resembled that of a bird, in so far as the main wings beat the air while the secondary ones, like a spread-out tail, balanced and helped direction; whereas in most (every so far I have noticed) butterflies' both sets of wings beat the air. I shall probably come across many other exciting things like this before I leave this country.

A friend and I got the chance to go into a country town S. We were walking up the street when we spotted on a small bookstall a paper in Indian writing and a large picture of Harry (!)* on the front page.

One fellow said yesterday, "I wish the bloody war would end." I jumped down his throat with the comment, "I wish it would begin, then it will end quick enough." But one never quite gives up hope that one day the news one longs above all to hear will come on the air—Allied forces have landed on the continent of Europe.

February 13, 1943. On the move
Sometimes I have the most penetrating and painful realizations of the utter negativeness of my own existence here. When we are on the road in lorries and we pass a convoy of peasant bullock carts loaded up with heavy stones, huge logs, etc., I sometimes

* Harry Pollitt.—*Ed.*

long to give them our trucks. For, after all, they build, while we kill. How often I have thought of providing every well with a petrol pump—the cost would be a mere spoonful from the torrent of war. I am feeling grand—pretty fit, sleeping out. I wish I could tell you something of my present activities—but I mustn't, for security reasons.

February, 1943. Karwar

This and the next few letters will be in the form of a diary, as we are moving about. After several days of interesting and, at times, hard work, we have arrived here, Karwar, after an all-night drive through real primary jungle. I didn't sleep a wink but sat and thought. Among other things I wondered what is the explanation of the fact that so many plants have prickles. This is not meant to be funny. We have here an inanimate object—a vegetable—developing weapons of a really powerful order. One can understand an animal or insect developing weapons of attack and seizure. But can one say that a plant (with no brain or nervous system) consciously develops sharp and strong prickles, tendrils, to prevent the encroachment of animals who might tread on it? I shall have to think about this some more.

We arrived here soon after dawn. How to describe it? A beautiful stretch of sand, a gentle sea, palm trees, a fishing community, and warm. In fact, just the place one would love to see turned into a rest home for the thousands of peasants one has seen toiling on the dry soil, or the workers in the mills. A really perfect place for such a purpose. I bathed to get some of the dust off. Then slept for a couple of hours and then went for a walk along the beach with a friend. How very, very much I wished I had a paint box. If we ever get the chance of coming to India in a civilized way we will visit here.

When the sun set this evening, it turned a brilliant vermilion, its roundness absolutely clear. It went down so slowly as to cause no splash on the sea—but rather floated. The ancients believed that a boat took it round to the East for the next morning. At the same time the sea went pale viridian green—the sky a cold transparent mauve and the sandy shore ivory. The fishermen, more black than ever, were in their black boats, adjusting their nets

51

which were stretched out into the water and hanging on long poles. In the next letter I will have a small drawing of this. Across the sun, horizontally to emphasize its floating, were three streaks of madder and its shape was as though its own weight lay on the water level, and so huge as to dominate the whole background.

February, 1943. Karwar

Today we went out woodcutting. During the expedition we came across two native woodcutters who cut up two trees for 8 annas each—they were superb at their craft, both with an axe (with a head that is proportionately longer than our usual ones) and with a curved knife. On our way back we stopped by a religious chariot —a huge mass of deeply carved woodwork on heavy wheels. This Indian woodcarving has a magnificent weight about it. Yesterday evening I went into the "town." Not at all interesting but for the schools and public library, most beautifully kept and with quite a number of good books.

This morning I bathed before breakfast. In a recent letter I described some peasant carvings. Recently I found a toy cat, home-made of wood, and some little stone objects, which I am keeping. From time to time fellows look at them. One chap yesterday solemnly informed me it was unlucky to have them. I asked him why he thought so. He replied that he once had one, and two months after he had a serious motor accident. Incredible, isn't it, for 1943? These old sweats with long service in India are full of such stuff about everything Indian. Sir James Fraser has some excellent material on such "magic" at the beginning of *The Golden Bough*.

I went at 5 o'clock to watch a game of hockey against the local boys' high school. After the game, which was a very good one, I had a quick look at the school. It had some quite up-to-date scientific instruments. In the museum room there was a good collection of birds, snakes and fish caught by the pupils.

When we got back to camp and had had some supper, a number of students came round to invite us to go for a walk and talk with them. I am very excited about this, as I have carried on, almost alone, a battle on this question—that Indians are human beings. Now a whole group have discovered this to their amazement and

52

pleasure, as they have now lost quite a lot of feeling of exiles. On the walk we had a good discussion on the incorrectness of the Congress policy. It is quite clear that (1) the youths are thinking hard, because Congress has got them nowhere; (2) that British Imperialism is so hated that it represents fascism—their emotional —*i.e.,* national—outlook, which is very strong both as Indians and workers, so hopelessly predominates that they are almost blind to the international basis of prerequisites of Indian independence.

An interesting incident in connection with all this is that one of the fellows who has been talking to these students made the announcement that in his opinion these Indians are far more intelligent than English youths. This discovery has thrilled him— "Think what that means with 100 millions of them," he says, with eyes alight, and then adds, "It is almost terrifying." His discovery is but half-way towards a full understanding of what independence *does.*

Today I shall spend wandering about looking with notebook and pencil. It is so very beautiful here that I would love to spend some time painting. There is an artist, Indian, who lives here. I am trying to get to know him in the hope of arranging for my next leave.

February, 1943. Karwar

Yesterday I shall remember for a long time. The local boys' school headmaster invited one of our fellows to give a talk to the 4th, 5th and 6th forms and staff on "English Education." He invited me to go along with him and his friends, in all a party of six. Imagine six British soldiers being invited to an Indian school to speak on Education—and imagine six British soldiers heartily accepting the offer.

It was a roaring success. He spoke in English for about 15 minutes, and then question time. Questions were invited on *all* subjects. Many were on education itself, but some of the boys asked such questions as "Do you learn Indian history at school?" "What is the essence of English patriotism?" "What are your impressions of India as compared to England?" "Britain has ruled India for 150 years—if India conquered Britain, how long would it rule?" I was asked by the six others to give the replies to these and other such questions, and I took as my guiding rule a people's program—national unity, liberation of women, universal education, etc. The meeting lasted over an hour and was enjoyed by everyone. What struck us most was that the whole thing was done in English. Imagine such a thing happening, say, in French in an English school with pupils aged 11 to 14! The brightness and intelligence of these children is splendid.

After the meeting in the school, we went for a walk along the seashore with a number of the pupils, when we discussed all sorts of things. This morning I am due to take a class, Standard 5, on an English subject, and have chosen Wordsworth, for which they have lent me one of their school textbooks on English verse.

. . . Well, I got to the school where, after a wait of about 15 minutes, during which much arranging was going on between the headmaster and staff, I found myself in front of practically the whole outfit, including the staff. Incidentally, boys *and* girls. I was given an hour, but took three-quarters of an hour, and the rest on questions. I made the work of Wordsworth my theme, and around this spoke on the elements of poetry—sound, rhythm, etc., of words—the influences of Wordsworth—1789 and industrialism —commerce—the message of Wordsworth—a healthy, youthful love of nature and a people's poetry. Then I read them some of the poems—Westminster Bridge, Milton, etc. The questions included who was the greater, Milton or Shakespeare, and why?— questions about the 20th century English poets, how exactly did Wordsworth react to the French Revolution?—what new things did he impart to English poetry? etc., etc. Isn't it perfectly clear that these ignorant wogs are not fit to govern themselves? The headmaster was extremely grateful to me for doing this, as though *they* were the ones to benefit! It was marvelous for me to be among them.

This evening the squadron plays them at football, and myself and my colleague have been invited to tea with the staff. Tomorrow we leave here early.

I can say of Karwar that it is one of the loveliest places I have ever seen. I shall never forget these fishermen, these peasants, these children and their little town.

. . . In the afternoon, at 4:30, my friend and I went along to the

54

school, where he gave another talk on the English universities. After this we two had tea with the headmaster and staff—tea, two little bananas and some mixed-up nuts and ginger—all standing round a table. At 6 o'clock I met three boys from a Hindu school and had a really interesting talk with them.

All the time at Karwar I had a curious idea running through my mind—one that is the theme of Barrie, *Thunder Rock*, not to mention others—*i.e.*, that I coming, literally out of the blue, should speak to them on what Wordsworth said to me over a hundred years ago. As though space were catching up on time.

Part II: At the Gunnery School

Please note the address. A most extraordinary thing has happened. Two days ago my name appeared on orders as War Posted to the Gunnery Wing, Ahmednagar. So I am here, possibly to become an instructor-sergeant. It will mean some good hard work for the next few months. So we kill two birds with one stone. One, I have a chance to achieve my ambition in the army career—to become a sergeant-instructor in a technical branch. And two, I am now in the place where I was born! . . .

I was very touched by a number of conversations, etc., I had before I left the regiment. I have promised to look up a fellow, L. B.——, after the war. I made great friends with him over the past year, a very intelligent and honest bloke who is reading a great deal.

The food is good here—I shall have to take great care not to grow into a tub. Fortunately the wing I work in is a little way from where I sleep, so I shall have some walking to do. On the radio Frank Owen is just about to talk about the R.A.C.!! We are all ears to hear what it is like inside a tank. *Oh, yeah?* He says: "Driving a tank across country is like riding a horse." When will such drivel be stopped? The cavalry tradition that pervades the R.A.C. is the poor tankist's nightmare. Tanks are tanks, and NOT horses. One day we'll learn.

I am settling in and learning the ropes. I have to do much preparatory work now in order to be ready for teaching. Today is Sunday. And of course, as is the case when war is far away, compulsory church parades have been started. An army parade of detailed men to church is really the most vile abuse of freedom of men's intelligence ever invented. The men loathe it—their contempt for the Church increases. So much is this the case that

56

those men who go voluntarily very often refuse to attend such a service where fellows are forced to worship. In England the mockery is bad enough where there is a friendliness among the general people—but here in India, where the mass of humanity are treated as though they were nothing more than beasts, one cannot tolerate the hypocrisy of it all.

As soon as I can I shall go into Bombay to get some good books and try to meet some people, otherwise I shall become stale, flat and unprofitable. Fortunately in the modern arm of the Army—tanks —one is helped to keep sane by continual contact with machinery, and still more by contact with the real technicians, the drivers, gunners and operators. These people have no romantic ideas about things, they don't confuse tanks with horses, they don't mix up a shouted command with the technical job of making the tank go. Back in the regiment one was always helped by the constant company of such people—I hope it will be the same here.

March 10, 1943. Ahmednagar

I have made an encouraging start here, attached to a class of officers. Almost on my arrival here I got talking to a fellow— Jewish lad from Streatham—who eventually produced some fairly recent copies of *People's War*. I was very glad as I had not seen a copy for some weeks. But I am looking forward very much to my next leave as I want to get up-to-date.

The food situation is still serious in spite of the fact that the bureaucracy has the matter well in hand. The following quotation from an article in the Illustrated Weekly of India, in the form of question and answer helps us to understand.

Q. But isn't it a fact that within a very short time of price control being lifted 60,000 tons of grain were bought in the Punjab markets compared with a mere 8,000 previously?

A. Yes, that seems to be the case, and selling having started— of course at a much higher price than the controlled figure— hoarded stocks are reported to be pouring into the markets . . . so that the rate has now started to fall.

This is how the Government solves the food crisis!

57

Compare this with the people's method led by the C.P.I. as at Nileswaram in Kasargode Taluk. Here our comrades got reliable information about the secret hoarding of sugar by some merchants. They persuaded the Deputy Talisildar to search a tea shop. Four bags of sugar were found hidden behind a stack of firewood. They also found a hoard of small coins (a scarcity of these was created as part of the fifth column activities, by the way). In another shop they found 15 bags of sugar. And so on, still on a small scale, but a real beginning on an issue which the people feel.

How stupid Gandhi's fast looks compared to the grandeur of a handful of Indian peasants and workers uniting to demand their human rights! No wonder the Viceroy corresponds with Gandhi and sends the police after the people. Of course, Halifax, with eyes to Heaven and hands in his pockets has written in *The American* that "we continue to regard India as a trust, and not a possession." We are slowly drifting once more to the white man's burden standpoint. But you can rest assured that it is no mere theory that India will not put up with being a subject nation for much longer. History is, in its inevitable way, bringing the paths of national independence and socialism to meet into one great modern highway to the future.

Today three little Indian children stood watching us at work on a tank. One of these was very, very young—but could stand up. He was making baby noises for speech and in every way behaving as very tiny children do. I could not help watching him. Then, suddenly, one of the older children noticed I was looking at the baby and so immediately told the little kid to "salaam the soldier sahib." This not only made me angry but absolutely disgusted. On our regimental orders yesterday appeared a paragraph to the effect that British other ranks had been observed treating the Indian truck drivers in a wrong manner. They must remember that these Indian drivers are not civilians but soldiers like themselves, advised the higher-ups. One feels like and is treated like some bloody Nazi in India when in this uniform.

In India, as in every country, there are famous shrines, temples and what-not—Taj Mahal, for instance—which claim the attention of tourists and history. To these it is explained that the great

58

warrior so-and-so had this built, or that Prince Kitua-Budley-Hai built this shrine to his mistress Tora Peachy. Now, in fact, these swine did not build these things at all but had the power to force the people living in hovels and filth to use their labor and skill to these ends instead of sanitation, common housing, etc. And under imperialism this tendency is hopelessly exaggerated until the imperialists are wont to deny that an engine driver drives the train, but rather the big shareholder living across the seas. We are accustomed to an understanding of this in the vivid contrast of Battersea and Park Lane. But what we city folk often forget is that even underneath the engine driver, as the very foundation of his existence, is the incredibly hard and patient labor of millions of peasants, not only men but, owing to feudal and vicious religious influences, especially the women.

I shall never forget this lesson, so well taught at Nira Tank, (a holiday twice enjoyed and written about in my letters) where, in the great barrier wall holding in a lake of water, a plaque told how during the famine of —— year this water reservoir was built by so many thousand people as a relief measure. One could not but recall Shelley's magnificent sonnet, "My name is Ozymandias, King of Kings.... Look on my works, ye mighty, and despair.... The lone and level sands stretch far away," when one compared this work of irrigation built by the nameless, famine-stricken peasants of years ago with the utterly useless, self-glorification of "great" men. Thank goodness I came to India, even if only to see emphasized the proud durability of the work of the lowest strata of society, the peasant women, as against the pompous monument of the Imperial Army.

March 13, 1943. Ahmednagar

In a recent letter I raised a bitter howl *re* compulsory church parade. I am glad to say, so far as I can see permanently, these have been cancelled. In their place we are to spend between 9 and 12 cleaning up the barracks. This, in my opinion, is excellent. By the look of things, the new Brigadier is having a good clean-up in more senses than one—and from a newcomer's point of view, a good thing too.

This week has been a very hard one—looking at all I could see, making a really good notebook, and in general doing all I could to get the grade. Next week I have to give our Major a lesson, as a test, on stripping one of the guns—if I do it as well as I do it in my sleep (as a result of thinking of nothing else all day long) I shall miss becoming a sergeant and be promoted to a General straight away.

March 16, 1943. Ahmednagar

An editorial in the *Times of India* states: "Despite war and famine, the Punjab has another surplus Budget." And the editorial winds up with the point that proposals are afoot to spend certain monies on educational and medical services "which are badly in need of additional grants." A bureaucrat's dream! Famine and war, a balanced budget with surplus, and to follow, some expenditure on education and medical services *badly in need.*

The food situation should improve, as it is reported quantities of wheat have been imported from Australia—of course, as I pointed out in my last letter, the people will have to pay the difference between arresting profiteers and hoarders and imported grain. But from the point of view of the bureaucrat, the food shortage has been solved on paper, among the well-to-do at least.

I have had another good day in the gunnery wing. But I have a piece of really significant news from my room. A few days ago an old soldier hit the bearer—Indian batman to the men—with a leather strap. A corporal immediately put him on a charge and a number of the men expressed the view that after all the bearer is a human being. The fellow got seven days confined to barracks.

Slowly, very slowly, the old vicious attitude to Indians is going—but how slowly! Only last night I protested at a number of the men holding the tea-wallah's boy while inciting one of their dogs to bark at him. The boy is about nine years, if a day. This little piece of "fun" was being played because the kid had replied to an order to get some meat sandwiches from the canteen that he couldn't, as he was getting teas and cakes for other men. He was absolutely right—that is his job, and it is a busy one in the evenings. But again, I saw a Scotch lad give some sweets to two Indian bus drivers—the first time I have ever seen such a thing done and

60

the sort of thing for which I am always bringing indignation on myself.

Last week-end I got leave to Bombay. I went to see some friends, bought a lot of books—including the *Critique of the Gotha Program* and Dutt's *Britain and the World Front*—and, amazingly, ran into an ex-I.B.er* I shall see more of him if possible.

March 24, 1943. Ahmednagar

I was extremely pleased today when our new Major at the gunnery wing spoke to all the staff on various subjects, and included the following: "The ill-treatment of the Indians has got to stop—in future, anyone brought up on a charge for such an offense will be stripped (lose his rank) and severely punished—we are determined to put an end to the unpleasantness existing owing to such behavior." It was good to hear. There is no doubt that while some of the recent drafters have become "old soldiers," the bulk have been and remain extremely angry at this bloody-fascist relationship.

April 8, 1943. Ahmednagar

Here are two little items of news from India.

The Bengal cabinet resigned the day after the demonstration of 6,000 women in India (N.B.) had taken place in Calcutta—no mention of this appears in the press—demanding food.

The *Times of India* reports that the price of fish in Bombay has suddenly jumped 25 per cent because the I.C.I. has announced it cannot supply ammonia—for the manufacture of ice—so the ice manufacturers have to go to the black market for ammonia, for which they pay twenty times the pre-war price.

While I was in Bombay a week or so ago I wrote this poem:

BOMBAY

Come with me and I will show you,
Almost hidden in the shadow
Of an Indian night,
Pavements strewn with human bodies

* Member of the International Brigade in Spain.—*Ed.*

That with all the other shit
The authorities forget
Even to worry about.

Here's one
Still lives, though all his flesh has gone.
The vulture remains invisible
Till the meal is insensible,
But Life is not so patient as the vulture,
In India, not so poetical.

I also wrote the following poem, entitled "Ships."

SHIPS

I have leaned on the quayside of this world
And seen life glide inevitably away
On the ocean whose only horizon is
Unseen uncertain shore.

I've watched a galleon far to the edge of the West
Wait on the sea till the sun was lowered
Into the hold, and the rising darkness
Fill the sails for the East.

I have found deep in the sands of time
The skeleton of some long-buried ship
That in its prime split waves and like an arrow
Pierced storms to gain a fiord.

I have played with fragile sailing boats
Running round the pond's edge. Stood helpless by
Shipwrecks in miniature. And know the joy
Of reaching the far side.

I have been carried many weeks of miles
Well packed like merchandise for abroad
When only the thin shell of destiny buoyed
Soldiers to come back alive.

I have looked at crafts made by simple fishermen,
Built as they built them a thousand years past—
Long has that tiny village stood still
Karwar, against the tides.

I have walked aboard a liner so vast,
It felt as though I stood again on land,
Which barely swayed against the towering blast
Of huge collapsing waves.

From deck rails I have read the endless water,
As though my finger moved across a map
I searched in the wide expanse at my feet
The harbor I longed for.

But still I have one ship to travel by
It sails no seas yet brings an exile home
It goes no place yet needs a pilot. I
Would steer my people free.

Free from the chains that weigh the bows down,
Loose from the refuse that drags a blunted keel.
Clear decks for action! With steam and sail
Escape the dockside grasp.

Then we shall climb among the cliffs and breathe
Fresh winds fanned by the passing stars
And chart new courses for the ships we've dreamed
To ride the sky-deep seas.

April 13, 1943. Ahmednagar
  Since I last wrote you I have been in hospital for a week with a
touch of the fever. Two things happened of importance—I met a
nurse who had been in Spain and we had a long talk about things.
And as a result of meeting a bloke I hope to make arrangements
with an Art master who teaches in Ahmednagar to draw and
paint Indian models.   The negotiations are progressing.
  . . . Today has been a historic one for me. I went to the Indian
artist's house (mentioned above) and did a drawing for 1½ hours
of his little niece aged 10. I did it in indelible pencil and ink—

this is the medium I shall do most of my work in as it is more lasting—does not smudge—than ordinary pencil. But how very difficult are Indian clothes—I shall have to do a lot of careful observation and drawing before I shall know what to do technically. The Indian just sat and watched me working. He speaks English quite well, and knows a number of famous Indian painters—he himself went to the Bombay School of Art. He is going to give me an introduction to some Bombay artists when I go there on my next leave. You have no idea how lovely it was to draw again and how exciting to have an Indian as a model. He has promised to let me draw his family and arrange to get coolies, etc., as models. I look forward to a great time in the coming months—for this is what I really want to draw and paint—I shall try to learn water colors in the same way as when in the Italian concentration camp in Spain I learnt a lot about color through being compelled to paint in oils without white paint.

April 19, 1943. Ahmednagar

Today I finished the second of my large diagram-drawings for the gunnery wing. I did one of these at Dhond—they are really exciting to do, especially if one considers all questions of design, balance, color emphasis by contrast and mass. I shall start the third next month. I am working hard at this drawing work for two reasons—one, it is excellent practice in composing large surfaces of flat color and large line movement and, two, I hope to be given it as a job, apart from instructing, which really interests me.

I have done some real drawings of my artist friend's little baby daughter, 1 year old, his niece, 10 years, and an old, old woman. Next week I shall make some more drawings of the family, including him, and then set to work on a fair-sized family group in pen, pencil and water-color.

April 20, 1943. Ahmednagar

As you see, I am now a made-up sergeant. This week I have been extraordinarily happy owing to the drawing I am now doing with my Indian artist friend. I have been to his house three days running and every time have been met as a real friend. On Tuesday, after drawing, he took me round the market to see the peasants and look at the streets. Yesterday we went to see a photographer friend of his. I am learning so much about Indians—the people—they are extraordinarily friendly (no wonder the poor creatures find it difficult to believe that only an armed and long war will win independence).

Four peasants, lads and C.P.ers, were executed on March 29th for the crime of being organizers of a demonstration in Kayyur some time ago, during which a policeman was killed. Words fail one to express the level of cowardice of which the white sahib in India is capable. Thank goodness, you and I have been lucky enough to help build a human society instead of this society of jackals.

April 21, 1943. Ahmednagar

I am very excited because I have finished my Orderly Sergeant and I learn I am to have a squad to teach on a four weeks' course. This will be great, as for one thing I shall be learning a lot myself. My only regret is that I have not had a course myself so as to know the ropes.

The chief event of the week is that I have done drawings of every-one of the family of my artist friend.

This morning Dame History stepped in in the shape of the Major. "Would you be willing to be recommended for a Commission?" says he. "Yes," says I. So I shall probably be having an interview with the Brig. shortly.

Mark you, I don't necessarily take this as a recognition of ability. Members of the I.B. have sometimes been promoted only to gain the position of splendid isolation. We need not expect anything to be done about it for another three years at least—so don't get in a flap. As a matter of fact, a time lag will be useful to me to study the language—as you know my greatest weakness. I have picked up a phrase here and there, viz., "What the bloody hell's that?" translates into, "I say, old boy, can you put me in the picture?" (said in a tone of voice meaning, "I don't really want to know, you know, what"). Anyway, we shall see what happens, and in the meantime I shall do all I can to improve my technical military knowledge and my understanding of India.

You may regard the color of the stamps on this letter as symbolic —like the brilliant red flowers that decorated a lorry loaded with Indian laborers which went past me this morning on the way to the Gunnery.

I have said before that no sooner was the danger of direct Japanese invasion of India passed than the Government may very well make the Indian C.P. illegal again. The campaign is getting under way. A Central Committee member, Sardesai, is detained, Shukla in Kathiawar. District Committee men in Bengal. Party offices have been raided in Andhra and the Press in various localities (apart from paper restrictions) being fined, etc. On the 15th of last month, along with Sardesai, Yusuf, President of the Cawnpore Mazdoor Sabha and Kapur, the Secretary of the C.M.S. were arrested. The District Secretary, Banamali, is in jail. And so on.

The food situation doesn't seem to be as it was; in a large number of places People's Food Committees and Volunteers (People's Food Wardens) are springing up, preventing rioting and looting and getting, in many cases, the local authorities to act in a practical way, in contrast to the vast paper schemes adopted. In quite a number of places hoarders have been made to sell their stocks. It is mainly for this work that the Communists are being arrested. "For actively preventing rioting by urging positive action by the authorities against hoarders and black market," such is the crime deserving arrest perpetrated by many local Kisan (peasant) leaders (Patnaik in Padmapur) and local leaders (Reddy at Kurnool).

But even the authorities in some places are doing something. The *Statesman* reports today that during the week ended April 21st, 185 cases on charges of hoarding and profiteering were sent up for trial in Calcutta by the police and the inspecting staff of the Directorate of Civil Supplies. It was in Calcutta that a demonstration of women took place the day before the fall of the Huq Cabinet, over the food question.

May 12, 1943. Ahmednagar

The only piece of news of interest arises from a speech I have just read by Cripps, in England. He is reported to have told some Indians (industrial Bevin boys): "It is part of your job while you are here to study organization of labor so that you may, on your return to your own country, help your fellow workers to organize stable trade unions, not as political parties, but as protection for workers against exploitation and sweating and as a means of encouraging the sound development of Indian industries."

Would someone kindly inform Cripps that on May 1st, at Nagpur, the 20th session of the All-India T.U.C. met—300 delegates representing over 350,000 workers—and demanded, among other things, "as a protection for workers against exploitation" the transference of power to a national government. Also, on May 1st, the same day as Cripps spoke, railwaymen, tramwaymen, textile workers, etc., were organizing meetings in Bombay, Calcutta, Karachi, demanding, mainly, the opening of the Second Front. And above all, one should not forget the great Kisan (peasant) organizations. It is always a surprising fact to such "brilliant" legal minds as Cripps' that the ignorant workers and peasants, *in their own way,* arrive at an understanding of politics far in advance of their betters. And also tell Cripps it would make the organization of the workers much easier if Meerut trials and the imprisonment of men such as Dange and Mirajkar did not take place. "Safe" Labor leaders are not fashionable among ignorant Indian and Chinese workers.

May 17, 1943. Ahmednagar
Outside my bunk some building work has been started. Men and women laborers work together. The women bring their children—tiny babies to kids of six or seven. These are dumped down on some spot while the women work, carrying earth in flat bowls on their heads away from where the men dig, to dumps. Often one sees a little person, aged about one, wandering about among the workers. I have often thought how disgraceful it is that there are no schools or nurseries for these children. Today I happened to be in when these people knocked off. The overseer banged on a gong, and to my surprise everyone began talking, some cheered, and the whole scene changed from a machine-like motion to a collection of people. Amid much noise, talking and laughing, they collected their belongings—the women sat their children legs astride on their hips—handed in their bowls, picks, etc., and in

67

groups dispersed—presumably to their straw and mud-built huts which they call home. A sergeant said to me: "They're human after all—and should be treated as such. What I despise them for is for letting themselves be treated as badly as they are." (!)

These people work every day of the week at 6 annas for women, 10 annas for men per day.

Yesterday I had my interview with the Brigadier. One of the first questions was: "Have you a private income?" I answered NO, quite emphatically. I was so angry at having this question put that I spent the rest of a very short interview explaining I had no intention of becoming an officer. Today our Major tackled me, asking why I had turned down the commission. I explained that among the rank and file there was much ill-feeling against the officers because of this business of money, school tie, etc. I was still willing to become an officer on one condition, and one only—merit. That every time anything to do with money or class came into it I would turn it down flat. The Major said he was going to take up the matter again.

The *Times of India* for May 15th has two important articles headed: "Checking Rise in Cloth Prices" and "Main Causes of Food Shortage." In the first it is stated that "the prices of cloth have gone up by nearly 500 per cent from the pre-war level." The same article states: "The increase in prices of cloth is attributed to war conditions; speculative tendencies inherent in a war; the shortage of cloth and the lag between supply and demand; the increased cost of manufacture; and hoarding in anticipation of higher prices." "One prominent business man said that hoarding had become a habit" (!). "Prices of cotton piecegoods have risen so steeply that unless cheaper cloth is provided early, the poor and middle classes will be in a serious plight."

The Government is starting to do something about it. It is reported that Delhi has been allotted 500,000 yards of standard cloth for the quarter ending July 31st. About 45,000 persons are expected to benefit. (Note—It does not say whether these 45,000 persons are the Government agents, underwriters, purchasers on behalf of Government, wholesalers, retailers, Committee men in Bombay, Delhi, etc., banks, import agents, railways—not forgetting Tata and Wadia, paper manufacturers who supply the forms, printers, police, etc., etc., or the poor and middle classes, who number tens of millions!)

The article on food deals with a Conference in Bengal, attended by Government Bigwigs, who stressed: "Psychological factors were among the main causes for the shortage of essential foodstuffs and the rise in prices." Psychological is the new name for 6 annas a day, plus hoarding, plus profiteering, plus black market.

This week an event will take place in India of unique and immense importance—the Communist Party of India is holding in Bombay the first All-India Congress. The importance of this lies mainly in the fact that the C.P. now comes out publicly as a national, patriotic, united India leadership, just at a time when the Congress-Moslem sectarianism is being demonstrated in all its futility for the people of India. How I would love to be there— to hear these people working out plans for a people's India; and can't you imagine the Brig's face if I applied to go! "Sir. I herewith make my application to be absent from quarters from . . . to . . . to attend the All-India Congress of the C.P.I. in Bombay." Under the circumstances I don't think my application would be favorably received—even though the presence of British soldiers as friends at a conference of Indians would do an enormous amount of good as among the people of both countries.

In a recent letter, I made some comment on a speech by Cripps. I can now add that the All-Indian Trade Union Congress met at a time when more than 30 of the 62 members of its General Council are in jail—including its president, V. V. Giri. It was forbidden to hold an open session.

In Orissa, the legal C.P. has 35 members either in jail, on trial or detained. Incidentally, there are still famine conditions in Orissa following two cyclones of 15th and 16th October last year.

In the Punjab on April 1, 176 members of the C.P.I. were in jail, etc. Four Communists are still undergoing life sentences.

The position is utterly fantastic. The C.P.I. is the *only* Indian party organizing the peasants to grow more food—in the T.U.C. it was the Communists who fought for increasing production—the Communists day and night expose the actions of the Forward Bloc, the black market, etc. And still it is possible for the Jessore District Committee (Bengal) to be told in reply to a request to hold May Day celebrations that "meetings might be held only on condition that nothing political will be discussed at the meetings and that police officers should be allowed to attend the meetings to take down notes of the proceedings. Permission for taking out processions is refused."

May 23, 1943. Ahmednagar

Things are going ahead here at an amazing speed.

I have already referred to the C.P.I. Congress in Bombay. Joshi* in a statement to the press gives the following figures— membership 16,000 with direct leadership of 300,000 industrial workers, 400,000 *organized* peasants, 39,000 students, 41,000 *organized* women.

I can illustrate the meaning of these figures to you by taking a few recent happenings in districts. In Chittagong there are 38 Defense Committees with influence over 200,000 people of Chittagong. A central food committee is functioning. The Defense Committee controls 21 food stores and manages the rationing of food to 16,000 people in co-operation with the authorities. Food Committees in India play the same role as Production Committees in England.

I have just seen the report of the Kistra District Peasant Conference held on the 29th and 30th of April. 15,000 Kisans turned up, including 2,000 women and 2,000 agricultural laborers (depressed classes). The 2,000 women represented an organized 10,000 women. The Congress organized water supply, food for 10,000 people, a dynamo to supply electricity and operate loudspeakers, cattle shows, contests between draught bulls, competition between milch cows and, last but not least, the Burra Katha lasting about 4 hours. This latter is the traditional ballad form of Andhra but instead of the old heroes and gods, there appeared the poor peasants themselves, the Jap peril, etc.

This particular district Kisan organization did a job recently which with some other examples shows what a mess things are in. In 1942, certain waste land had been cultivated by the peasants without previous permission. The Revenue Department imposed

* P. C. Joshi, general secretary of the C.P.I.—*Ed.*

70

penalties amounting to as much as 8 times the water rate. The Kisan Sabha impressed upon the officials the contradiction between their grow-more-food appeals and the penalties. The penalties were withdrawn.

In the United Province, there is a dearth of bullocks. Due to indiscriminate slaughter of cattle by military contractors and their agents, Kisans are not able to get bullocks (normally worth Rs. 100 each, now cost Rs. 500). The local Kisan organization is demanding control of slaughtering or else the grow-more-food campaign will be a complete failure.

There are unbounded indications of inflation resulting in three and fourfold rise in prices of food, cloth, etc. The *main* cause of inflation has been the huge purchases made by the British Government on behalf of the army. These purchases are paid for in sterling in England against which the Government of India releases rupees—i.e., a huge increase in note circulation (there are also other causes, viz., black market, lack of stocks control, lack of price control, etc.). The Government, instead of allowing India to buy much-needed machinery in return, has decided to appropriate more of profits in the shape of E.P.T. There can only be one result of this in the absence of adequate labor laws and food and price control—increased black market, and an increased incentive for strikes. Such is the way the bureaucracy cures inflation.

I have before told of the women's movement in Calcutta and Bengal. On May 2 in Patua 2,000 women marched to a food rally. At Dindigal on April 18, 1,500 women marched in a food demonstration. In Gaya (Behar) 500 women attended a food rally on May 7. Following on the official introduction of rationing in Bombay, food committees are springing up everywhere to put into practice the rationing scheme. One can sum up by saying that a good beginning has been made by the masses to learn the lessons of the war, to implement democratic talk with appropriate action, and to weld people's unity. But the working class in Britain must at all costs prevent any further restrictions of Indian liberty.

June 2, 1943. Ahmednagar
The press reports of the C.P.I. Congress were quite good.

71

Among other things, Joshi said in his speech, "Hunger has done it (forged unity) better than anything else. Formulation of demands is not enough because they are patent. What is needed is a positive and wide building up of unity. To abuse the bureaucrat to please the patriot is to go the way the patriot himself went and out of which it is our task to rescue him. Verbal exposure of bureaucracy is satyagraha and not Bolshevism. It is to parade our helplessness and inability to win the people in support of Party policy."

And again, "Only if we act to solve the crisis within our country will others be able to help us."

He made a crystal clear analysis of the Congress dilemma and while on the issue of national defense stated, "Japan had entered the war for the domination of Asia. India was the biggest and easiest prize. The Japanese must either get India or see India being used as a base to wipe them out. The worse the situation for the Axis in the West, the more desperate the Japanese must become in the East and strike hardest at the weakest spot."

Referring to the campaign for the release of the Congress leaders he said, "An anti-repression campaign would be playing into the hands of the bureaucracy and not really working to get the leaders out. To get Gandhi out they should appeal to all to stop sabotage and explain that every bomb thrown was a bomb thrown at the leaders."

One would like to quote more, but there is not space. The program can be outlined as: (1) build people's defense of India and so build unity; (2) unite against hunger; (3) Congress accept principle of self-determination, League to demand release of leaders —so forge League-Congress unity without which both are helpless but with which added to (1) and (2) the aim of National Government becomes a practical possibility, and (4) India to play its full share in the people's world struggle for freedom.

Today's *Times of India* published a statement by Mr. Hydari, Secretary Department of Industries and Civil Supplies, in which the Government outlines a scheme to produce 2,000 million yards of cloth within the next 12 months and to sell it at controlled prices.

The statesman writes: "But while the situation regarding cloth

* A word here used to indicate Gandhi's policies.—*Ed.*

72

is considered manageable, the food problem continues to baffle the authorities. The Food Department's regional plan has not succeeded to the extent expected. . . ."

There is a movement away from the previous rapidly developing inflationary rise in the price of bullion.

A last piece of news—the all-Gujerat Trade Union Congress, which was to have been held in the first week of June, will not take place as the District Magistrate has refused permission for the Conference to take place.

June 8, 1943. Ahmednagar

Yesterday I had the good news that I am to have a squad to instruct on Monday. There is little other news—just routine. At the moment I am being bothered by what are called mango flies —tiny black flies that noiselessly dangle close in front of one's face —so light that the quick movement of one's hand only blows them away from one's hand.

An interesting scene took place at dinner. A sergeant came and asked, while he was sitting down, if we had heard that a native had been shot with a .22 rifle. We said no, and asked for more information. He was caught stealing a lettuce, was wounded and taken away in a bullock cart. A sergeant major then said: "Pity it didn't kill the bastard. One out of 400 million wouldn't be missed. Shoot the bloody lot of them." To my joy, two sergeants rounded on him vigorously. The one that brought the news— ex-middle east—saying that "They're human. I'd give the bloke that did it at least 5 years." The other sergeant took a more "historical" line. Neither were in the least moved by the subsequent and usual stories of how the frontier tribesmen treated prisoners. I was frightfully pleased and made no attempt to butt in.

It is most extraordinarily difficult to give any proper picture of India. Take for instance the sugar situation. A Press Note issued by the Government of India Sugar Controller's office says: "The sugar season 1942-43 is virtually over. While production has been unexpectedly good, dispatches from factories as on May 31 are as much as 45 per cent of the entire production, and the various provincial markets are well supplied. . . . 15,000 tons or 1.4 per cent of the entire production, are earmarked for export in 1943. . . ."

73

The *Times of India* replied: "Why then are Bombay's children limited to a totally inadequate five ounces of sugar a week (children under two receive no ration at all) and why is it necessary to make adults in the city choose between sweetening their tea and sweetening their food? In unrationed areas shortages and black markets are common." "We do not quarrel with rationing, for with hoarding and black markets rife it is undoubtedly the best way of ensuring that all share alike . . . the system of distribution requires a thorough overhaul."

Although the atmosphere is heavy with rain, the Monsoons cannot be said to have begun here—and I believe they are already late. Let us hope they don't fail as the crops will be destroyed and the food situation will be serious.

June 19, 1943. Ahmednagar

How I wish I could see a decent film. You should see the muck dished up to us, *One Foot in Heaven, A Night in the Tropics,* etc. Which reminds me that the only decent bookshop in Poona has now been made out of bounds to British troops. This week I started my squad—seven young officers—not a bad crowd.

During the last few days we have had some real rain, and in its wake some very tender grass has been sprinkled where only yesterday was parched earth. One wonders where it came from.

The *Statesman* has reported a resolution of the Lahore District of the C.P.I. demanding the release of the 700 Communists still in jail in India.

So Wavell is Viceroy! I would love to know what people at home think of this. At the moment a rather futile discussion is going on *re* the war—a sort of discussion of war strategy based on "facts" as expounded by the *Daily Express*—it just goes round and round like the music. May 1 was only yesterday, and nothing has happened to make it the middle of June.

Just outside my back door there are three children, two girls and one boy, working—lifting stones and arranging them. When I see those children working on a Sunday, and knowing what kind of houses they live in, knowing the education they *don't* get, all talk about religion, progress, civilization, stinks and turns putrid.

The major interviewed me at the beginning of the week and

said that he and the colonel were once more going to recommend me for an officer.

Bengal has recently seen the setting up of a Moslem League ministry—I have in previous letters told you of the background of the fall of the previous Huq ministry. Well, the League set to work *re* the food crisis. It has officially recognized the operation of people's food committees throughout Bengal in order to combat hoarding. This sounds very good, *but* Calcutta and Howrah districts are exempt from the scheme. Now it is precisely in these two places where the big commercial merchants hang out and have their hoards. The net result of the League's scheme is to launch the peasants against the little men and leave the big bastards to control the famine via the black market—such is the first practical application of the policy of Jinnah.

Here is a nice "gem" from a place called Tippera. Six Moslem students tracked down a hoarder and handed him over to the police. The police arrested the students and asked the hoarder to "quietly remove his stocks." The lesson is that you must not have only single party campaigns but a people's movement to shake up the bureaucratic machine. You may rest assured that the people of India are moving inevitably along the right road—learning from practical mistakes.

A sad thing happened two days ago when an Indian soldier was killed by accident during the assembly of a gun into a tank. I was told this by a sergeant who made it the occasion for a deeply felt opinion that we should not think of this as merely "another black bastard out of the way" but that he was a human being, with a wife and children, perhaps, etc. I was very pleased to be lectured to in this way—somewhat unusual.

July 5, 1943. Ahmednagar

It is pouring with rain. The earth is green and muddy, instead of the usual glaring dust. The sound of the water-drops falling from the gutters and the evening cries of the birds remind me so much of England.

I read today of Mr. Amery's speech on the maldistribution of food in India. This speech must be understood in concrete terms of bureaucracy, magistrates, police, black market, profiteers and hoarding—you can then see the actual movement of people's food committees kicking a state machine which by itself is too tied up with those responsible for the chaos to *do* anything. A new food conference is to be held soon in Delhi in view of the failure of previous plans!

I cannot put aside this letter without saying how excited I was to hear over the All-India Radio that the Party Congress in London had demanded a settlement in India. This made me feel ever so proud and brought up many close memories. But I am also sad because there is no one who was there who I can discuss it with.

July 10, 1943. Ahmednagar

Today I went into the Mess to look at a paper, and heard a sergeant say to a friend, "The jerries have begun their offensive." There came over me once again that feeling of combined anger and frustration that I felt over Spain and have felt ever since Dunkirk. I supose now we will "stand amazed" for the third time running at our heroic allies—present them with more golden swords—and make dozens of speeches reminding ourselves of Tunisia, etc., etc., *ad nauseam* till it makes one feel as ashamed as one did in those terrible days of Munich and Barcelona.

> ... Men condemned for years on end
> To suffer freedom to do nothing.
> The whitewashed sky is their cell walls
> And earth the floor they walk along
> To nowhere. Everything is theirs
> Trees, fields, birds, wealth, tanks, gems,
> So long as they don't do, don't think, don't
> Want to buy with their wages,
> Build with their hands and enjoy
> Life that is living. They've been warned
> "Who wants to take the storm up in both hands
> "And break this calm to smithereens
> "Shall go to prison." This dungeon echoes
> The song of birds, people's voices
> With the depths of fruitless nothingness,
> Emptiness, limitless space,

76

Where to do nothing by compulsion
"—a wolf clothed in a lamb's white skin—"
Is Freedom which compels men to do nothing.

At table there were a lot of cynical remarks all arising from the same feelings as I have. One sergeant from Lancashire said, "In Blighty last month were big maneuvers. Landing operations on grand scale. No, no joking. We took Blackpool from the Canadians." You have no idea how deeply angry the men are at the fact of thousands of soldiers sittng around both here and at home.

There was a piece of very good news from India. Another prominent Congressman recently let out of jail has made a statement to the effect that Congress must get working now on a positive program and must accept the responsibility for restoring the hopelessness that overhangs the mass of Indians as a result of negative policies.

July 12, 1943. Ahmednagar

How magnificent is the news from Sicily! Two fronts at last—I believe one is justified in saying this is really the beginning of the end—anyway the next few months will see some tremendous events in Europe.

I am just off for a week's leave in Bombay.

July 18, 1943. On leave in Bombay

I caught the train from Ahmednagar, and on arrival here tried to get a room at the Y.M.C.A.—full up. So I went around to the hotel where I have stayed before and am paying 12 rupees a day all-in. The first time I stayed here it was 6 rupees, and the last time, 9 rupees—now it is 12 and you can't get a room under. Even the Y.M. is double what it was when I first came to Bombay.

This morning I spent several hours with the comrades. We had a long discussion. I had a meal with them, Indian fashion, and wore sandals and no socks while I was there.

This evening I had a sad experience. It came about in this way. I saw an advert in a shop window of a lecture on the modern

77

Mahratti novel* organized by the P.E.N. Club. So I went, both to hear the lecture and at the back of my mind an idea that perhaps I might meet someone to talk with. The lecture was *excellent*. The lecturer took great pains to show the weakness of the novel lay (1) in mere imitation of the western novel; (2) divorce from actual people—for which he blamed both the novelists and social conditions; and (3) a continual preaching of what he described as Hollywood idealism alternating with morbidity, i.e., the theme; love—woman has child—marriage not possible because of social conditions—*but* social conditions being what they are and unalterable we must sympathize with immorality. Then we all came out and one of the audience—all were Indians except myself —pushed towards me obviously to speak to me, so I said, "Very interesting lecture—I enjoyed it enormously," He replied, "How was it you came—did you see a notice in the papers?" "No. I saw one in a bookshop window." "I was just wondering. It's strange to see a soldier at a meeting." And the whole thing dawned on me—in their minds I was a foreign soldier, in an army occupying their country, and therefore I must have been *sent* to the meeting. My answer didn't satisfy him in the least—not even when I showed him I wanted to learn about India—having read Tagore I wanted to read more. Whatever propaganda is put over here—and however much by an accident of history we may be on the side of democracy—Indians who think, know just what we are.

Well, I followed up the lecture by buying a little book produced by the P.E.N., called *Indo-Anglian Literature*. On p. 43 it describes Mulk Raj Anand—actively connected with the All-India Progressive Writers' Association—the author of various books, viz., *Coolie, Untouchable, The Village*. I thought to myself, here at last is the kind of book I want about Indians. So I go to two of the largest bookshops. They tell me politely they have none of his books in stock, and then one blurts out: "The Coolie is banned." I was livid with anger. You can buy Hitler's speeches, you can buy *Mein Kampf,* the autobiography of Bose; you can buy everywhere filthy literature and filthy photographs—but novels

* A novel about the people living in the western part of India.—*Ed.*

about the Indian people by a progressive Indian writer are *banned!*
Words fail one sometimes to describe the hypocrisy of the British
ruling class when they pose as the champions of culture and
democracy.

The fifth column are becoming much more active. Chandra Bose
is in Singapore and broadcasts as the "Commander-in-Chief of the
Army of Liberation." He has already spoken of paratroops to be
dropped in Indian clothes and appealed to the peasantry to give
them cover. Meanwhile the Congress Socialists and Trotskyists are
using the absence of Congress leadership in jail, and the frightful
distress caused by famine, soaring prices, etc., plus the hopeless
ineffectiveness of the Government's bureaucratic schemes, to incite
to riot, strikes, and so on.

Only an idiot will think (and plenty do) that the Japs are going
to sit tight until the war is over. And what could guarantee victory
for the Japs more than the leaderless masses of India in the grip of
food crisis? Prominent people talk of finishing Japan in anything
from after 1945 to 1949. Their policy is based on drift in India,
Japanese inaction, pending the transfer of war strength from
Europe to India. But drift in India will soon enter the period of
riotings and strikes. Only the C.P.I. is holding it back now. The
release of Congress leaders to tackle the crisis is fundamental to our
beating the Japs soon and thoroughly. I write of this with very
great personal feeling.

July 20, 1943. On leave in Bombay

There have recently been a number of proposals by leading Congressmen (Srivastava in particular) to call on A.I.C.C. to withdraw
the August Resolution. There are very strong rumors that Gandhi
has written again to the Viceroy proposing that he be allowed to
meet members of the A.I.C.C. now in jail, to officially withdraw
the August Resolution so as to end the deadlock. Now these moves
by the higher-ups are of course parliamentary maneuvers—i.e., we
failed, we are in jail, we're stuck, so let's make a retreat and start
again along new lines—after all we must be realists—etc. But *below*
this, among the workers, the people, there is a process of learning
from events—famine and prices—taking place. Famine has imposed the necessity of food committees. Add to this the cotton-

79

owners' sabotage of cloth control and the big bosses' (British included) revolt against increasing wages to meet the cost of living, plus the complete incompetence of the Government to operate any scheme without the aid of the people (whom they are against!), and you get the forces operating which today are resulting in the workers, railwaymen, etc., taking up a very positive line to production—i.e., production committees. In other words, the negative line of Gandhism is slowly being understood and a positive policy is now being forged. This process is so vast—400 millions are affected—that there are bound to be mistakes, false starts, etc.

Here is a story which will illustrate the profound political change taking place.

Malabar is a district where cholera is raging—in Calicut, within one month, 704 people had it, of which 608 died; in Thanur village, 155 deaths occurred in one week; Tirur Range, 55 deaths in two days, and so on. In the town of Cananore cholera broke out. On June 26th, only three cases had been reported, but already the fifth column was around saying that nothing could be done about it—the bureaucracy was to blame—and that the people should disperse to the villages.

The Taluk C.P. arranged a meeting of Party members to hear two doctors give a talk on how to prevent the disease spreading. Next day 40 C.P.ers in eight squads visited 793 houses to explain to the people how the epidemic could be stopped. (Dr. Tampy would not allow more to go out as only 40 could be inoculated the first day.) On July 4—a Sunday—180 Red Guards with carts, brooms, spades, etc., went out to four separate parts of the town and started clearing up the refuse dumps, drains, streets, etc., etc., and all the while shouting anti-cholera slogans. The people saw—and did! Everyone joined in. They fetched their own implements from their houses and joined the Red Guards. Now the Chirakkal Taluk Cholera Relief Committee has been formed—Congress, Moslem League, C.P. and doctors.

From Cuttack in Orissa comes another story. On June 28 the Legislative Assembly met. The Premier, the Maharaja of Parlakimedi deplored the shortage of food. The stock of rice had disappeared. The price per bag had risen from RS.19/8 to Rs.23/8. He blamed the Central Government. Congress members blamed the Ministry and "called upon the Ministry to resign and lay the consequences on the shoulders of the bureaucratic Government." But the Food Committee of Cuttack led 2,000 hunger marchers (including 500 women) to the Assembly with five simple demands: (1) All parties unite to solve the food crisis; (2) Accept the co-operation of the people; (3) Stop indiscriminate exports of rice; (4) Rice rate to be reduced to Rs.8/ per maund; (5) Rice to be rationed to eight chataks, or 105 tolas per head per day. *Result*—the Maharaja promised rationing as from July 1, and the District Magistrate, immediately *on the spot*, distributed 50 maunds of rice (about 4,000 lbs.). The people are beginning to learn the bankruptcy of the policy of apportioning blame only—are beginning to learn the positive policy of unity for the practical solution of their problems. There is now a paper shortage, so the students in Bengal are making their own paper.

This sort of thing shows how much we can rely on the Indian people, in spite of the bloody awful mess being made by the fifth column, the Government and the profiteers, etc. But such actions are not yet universal—mainly owing to the fact that the Communist Party is frowned upon by the bureaucracy—hundreds are still in jail.

A last tidbit for Cripps—the South Indian Railway Workers' Union in June, 1943, had a membership of 20,000 out of a total of 35,000 workers. It has won the 8-hour day and Sunday holidays for gangmen. It has its own printing press. It has won its demand for grain shops. And at its recent annual conference, along the back of the platform, it had four huge portraits—Engels, Lenin, Stalin and Marx. One can see why Cripps' advice is so badly needed by the union—a resolution banning members of any political party from holding office received only five votes. Comrade Ranadive of the Communist Party of India presided.

The *Times of India* reports: "Prominent citizens of all parts of Dahm Taluka have evolved a scheme of voluntary rationing of sugar, kerosene and standard cloth, and to sell them to the public at controlled rates." These and hundreds of other examples will show you what would be meant by a National Government.

One could so easily degenerate into the attitude of the regular soldier or pukka sahib, if the only India one could see was *official*

81

India—Colville, Tata, the Maharajas, etc. Yes, that India is nowhere near capable of self-government, of independence. But there is another India, an India of the people, the workers and peasants; an India of intellectual giants like the Bengal girl, Toru Dutt, who died at the age of 21 after having written original poetry in English and translated French poetry into English; like Tagore; like Sarojini Naidu;* like thousands of Indians who are gulping down all that they can seize from the culture of the West, East, Past and Present. It is these facts that keep one's spirit alive and upon which is based the *immediate* practicability of Indian Independence Now.

July 23, 1943. On leave in Bombay

In my last letter I spoke of the activities of the fifth column—the following illustrates the situation:

A month ago the Government passed its cloth control ordinance, and a Control Board was set up to operate it. Out of 25 seats, 15 go to the millowners of Bombay, Ahmedabad, etc. Two seats are held by financiers of textiles and transport. Five seats to traders and distributors. *One* of the remaining three goes to Labor (i.e., to the general secretary of the All-India T.U.C.).

The Control scheme is to counter the policy of high prices and no cloth of the millowners, financiers, traders and distributors. But there is *no one* on the Board representing the consumers. Not content with this, the millowners occupied completely the most important sub-committee of the Board—the one dealing with fixation of prices and production—and put the one and only Labor representative on the Exports Committee. *And the Government have agreed!* Yet it has been demonstrated a thousand times in the last twelve months that without the people no scheme to deal with food, prices, etc., will be anything other than one more chance for the profiteers, fifth column, etc., to work havoc with the security of India.

The way that the cloth scheme will go is already becoming clear. For example, the Government did for a time get the wholesale price of cloth to drop—result, certain firms bought it up cheap for export

* An Indian woman poet.—*Ed.*

82

on behalf of the United Kingdom Commercial Corporation—and the price of cloth to the people remains where it was.

The attitude of the various sections concerned is shown by the following incident from the Bombay mills. The millowners said they would soon have to close down mills because of the shortage of electricity. The Government proposed a staggering of holidays so that the mills could work on Sunday. The millowners, not wanting to keep the mills going, so as to maintain scarcity and high prices, made the excuse that the workers would strike at Sunday work on the proposed lines. The reply quickly came from Dange of the Girni Kamgar Union and members of the T.U.C. that the workers had agreed to operate staggered holidays. So on the 18th of July the millowners were forced to open 58 mills.

But the millowners also resorted to the following in the name of the sacred right of Sunday holidays: Toadies, clerks, blacklegs, etc., all became great leaders of working-class struggle overnight. The Kandalkar gang of saboteurs and blacklegs and fifth columnists issued thousands of leaflets inciting to strike action. (Note, the union cannot afford to issue leaflets as the price of paper is prohibitive—the only cheap paper is to be got on the black market.) Gangs of thugs went out to intimidate with knife-stabbing (a method now being used on the leaders of the Bombay students' union by the fifth column in their efforts to get another campaign of sabotage like in August last year). The Girni Kamgar Union wanted to retaliate to this propaganda—but such leaflets as they had were not allowed in the factories, and the Government Labor Officer refused the use of certain big maidans* for meetings on a feeble excuse.

On the fateful Sunday, what happened? At the Morarji Gokuldas mill (the son of the owner of which was arrested for suspected sabotage and released on signing a document) men were planted at the gates with knives to assault and molest women operatives. At the Moon, the Jubilee Mills, the managers, the clerks, head-jobbers, etc., stood at the gates and turned back the workers. All told, by various means, eleven mills "struck" in defense of Sunday holidays. Forty-seven mills worked!! Once

* Open spaces.—*Ed.*

83

again the workers have shown themselves against sabotage. But have the millowners been arrested? Not on your life—they're all on the Cotton Control Board "to produce more cloth at lower prices."

In Bombay, milk prices have risen—June, 1942, 6 annas per ser; February, 1943, 8 annas per ser; March, 1943, 10 annas per ser. The milk trade interests shout "cattle food is scarce." Price of fodder *has* risen Rs.25/ per 1,000 lbs. in November, 1942, to Rs.65/ in February, 1943. Note, however, that a powerful ring of milk finance also operates on the fodder market. But also, contrary to the milk trade interests, the following are facts: When fodder rose to Rs.65/ the Government released its stocks of fodder, which brought the price down to Rs.38/ per 1,000 lbs. But far from the price of milk dropping, *it is still going up.* Then comes another excuse—the army must be fed with meat and milk—but no one can show that the killing of cattle increase is anywhere near sufficient to account for the present rise in milk prices. The fact of the matter is that for years past the milk trade has been in the hands of the big cattle owners, who therefore control quality (which is disgraceful) and prices. Here again, if the Government start a scheme for control of milk (and as far as I know they have not yet done so), it will be no use at all unless the people are taking part in it.

In Gwalior, the Gwalior State Congress Party has withdrawn its support of the August Resolution. The result is that all the Congressmen have been released from jail in Gwalior State and the Sarvajanak Sabha (Gwalior Congress Party) is now once again a fully legal organization.

In Lucknow a People's Food Conference was held—to cover the whole district—on July 4, presided over by a Sjt Scrivastava, Congress. The Secretary of the U.P. Moslem League and the Secretary of the Lucknow Moslem League Defense Committee were present—also Hindu Sabha, Central Sikh Dewan, Merchants' Association. At Hyderabad the same kind of thing.

And as a symptom of how deeply the movement is rooted everywhere, the women are on the move. In as yet a naive way very often. For instance, at the South India Railwaymen's Union Conference—at which there were 500 delegates and all the leading positions in the hands of the proletarians proper (instead of clerks,

84

postmasters as previously)—some of the delegates brought along their families, wives, daughters, etc., and these women were furious because they weren't allowed to vote as well as the men.

There is also another lovely story from this Railwaymen's Conference. At an important rail workshop employing 5,000 about 4,500 are union members. Ranadive, not a member of the Union, was the president at the Conference. The railworkers know Ranadive of old and love him. The Conference was a tremendous success. When all the decisions had been taken, after three days of speeches, and talking, the workers felt themselves stronger. They wished to do great honor to their comrade Ranadive. So they invited Ranadive to see round their workshops. It must be said that at these works much of the production is for war purposes and to look round you have to possess a special pass. Ranadive had no pass. But the workers took him in and conducted him round their respective shops. While going through one shop, where the work was on war material, Ranadive and his guide were stopped. A British captain rushed up and asked, firmly, in English, "Where is your pass? You have no right to come here without authority." Ranadive, not quite clear what to say, translated the Captain's words to his guide. And without hesitation the Indian railworker looked up at the British Officer Sahib and replied, "Ranadive is a member of the Political Bureau of the Communist Party of India." And he led Ranadive on through to the next department.

Don't you think that is a marvelous story?

July 25, 1943. Ahmednagar

I am now back in Ahmednagar. On my last day in Bombay I went round to some friends where among lots of interesting talk (1) I gave an outline of the history of the Labor Movement in England with special reference to the basic meaning of "I'm a Labor man"; (2) I met the (Censored) who has just been to S. India, including Madras, and he talked to me for over an hour on things in S. India; and (3) in the evening an Indian lady, the wife of one of my friends, played music on an Indian mandolin-like instrument and we had a long discussion on types of Indian music as well as on the traditional cultural forms—musical (vocal) epic recitation—so loved by the Indian peasantry—forms into which the *new* poets are putting new content. I was told of an occasion when 20,000 peasants sat motionless for six hours—these peasants cannot sit for more than a half hour's speechifying.

The last few days I felt rather rotten, but I was lucky in being able to lie down the whole train journey back. An Indian, whom I had never met before, insisted on buying me, at great inconvenience to himself, some sandwiches at one of the stations.

Yesterday I had another interview with our Major—my letter of the 18th has been somewhat censored apparently, exactly how much I am not sure. But that was the cause of the interview. The main points were: (1) That the letter had gone higher up than the Major. (2) That the authorities know what I am from my military documents. (3) *Re* Bose in Singapore—where did I get the information—did I listen in to his broadcasts (!!). (4) Did I feel I had enough work to do. I won't bother to deal with 1, 2 and 4 as they are clear enough to you, but in case you have any doubts about 3 all the news I send that is not direct personal experience comes from the *Times of India, Statesman* and *People's War* as well as, unfortunately far too seldom, a result of any conversation with responsible people.

Anyway, an excellent thing has happened now—we have officially, as part of our training, to have one period a week given up to current affairs. This week an officer, speaking from the book, dealt with the question: "Why we fight the Japs." Here are the answers: (1) Because we are going to prove that the old chatter about the Empire being rotten and breaking up is not true. We shall show that the Empire is still very powerful. (2) We must not desert the Australians in the face of Jap threat. (3) We have to regain lost possessions. (4) From a sense of revenge for the dirty methods of war used by the Japs. (5) to re-establish international law and order.

It doesn't need much intelligence to understand that such war aims find the coolest sympathy among the millions of Chinese, Indians, Burmese, etc., and among quite a large number of British soldiers. But that does not mean these "others" don't want to

86

fight the Japs—*on the contrary*, they have the most profound desire to fight Japan—in order to annihilate fascism, in order to mobilize the peoples for such a war, in order to win the demands of the Atlantic Charter which says absolutely nothing about empires, but on the contrary speaks of the *independence of nations*. We are not all bound to have sympathy with fascism just because the most respectable newspaper in India (the *Times of India*) again, within a week, *editorially* proclaims that "fascism in its early stages in Italy was a good thing."

The immediate result of the interview was a fit of depression and a bad night's sleep. I am not so tough that I can get over these reminders of reality easily—I remember that I was fighting fascism *voluntarily* years before 1939—yet *I* am the one who is watched, who is not allowed promotion, simply because I demand an all-out effort against fascism by those who today pretend to be fighting for freedom, and because I get angry when the books of progressive writers are banned while the works of Hitler, Bose, etc., are on sale.

But today I feel better again. For I am only a speck compared to the vast millions of humanity on the move. Soon it will not be necessary to write to you about the actions of a few people as news. The stage is now being reached when millions of humanity are starting to act. And I think by all signs India is not so far behind Europe. When one lifts up one's head to look around, yesterday's interview can be seen to be neither a world historic event, nor anything to be unduly miserable about. One must just keep on to the best of one's ability becoming an efficient soldier, learning more and more about the common people, increasing one's hatred for their enemies. What times to be living through—how *incredibly* lucky we are to witness millions and millions of people getting up off their knees before Gods, Kings, "Leaders" and Empires—to stand upright as men and women. How very small one feels, and yet how very happy to be one of them.

July 29, 1943. Ahmednagar

It will be so very soon the end of another month, and another month after that I shall be 36. But now things are reversed. Before time flew and nothing happened—now in a matter of hours a nation decides to throw away the past. Now time has to hurry to keep events in sight. I have just read Churchill's speech. It makes one thing clear—the Italian *people* did the job.

August 3, 1943. Ahmednagar

There is no news from the F.V.S. except that we are now getting fresh green peas in the Sergeants' Mess.

Two members of the A.I.C.C., Sabbarayan and Srivastava, have declared their intention of convening a meeting of all A.I.C.C. members out of jail to review the present situation. It was Srivastava who recently declared in favor of rescinding the August Resolution. This is excellent, as it shows initiative is being taken, *apart from* Gandhi (not against, mark you). I have not the slightest doubt the Indians will achieve a fighting unity in due course—I say a fighting unity because based on the antagonism of classes (the peasantry led by the proletariat) in contrast to the sort of official mush envisaged here—Princes, plus Tata, plus Aga Khan, etc., etc.

I have just seen today's *Times of India,* in which there are two articles on the extremely serious (in degree and extent) famine in Bengal. (There is still no rationing in Calcutta as, for instance, in Bombay.) Rice in some parts of the country is at Rs.8 to 15 per maund, but in Bengal at Rs.30 to 35. Recently the Bengal jute mills ceased production for a week to give time for a Government scheme reorganizing the coal supplies. One week proved useless, so they have stopped for another week. Now the cotton bosses declare that the shortage of coal is preventing mills from working—some have closed down, others curtailed production.

Bengal legislators are demanding the Government declare the whole of Bengal, tens of millions, a famine area. There is absolutely no means of saving India without rousing the Indian people—and Viceregal sermons, however correct, *re* Indians, will not and cannot replace the urgent necessity of *action* to unite the Indians. There have got to be two things: (1) Government control of prices and rations; (2) a government that can do the job in one. I am not in any sense suggesting the need for panic—what I have in mind is the contradiction between a war policy which proposes to deal with Japan in due course while the situation is rapidly deteriorating throughout *the base* of operations, India. I must not write any more than this because it will probably be censored. But the situation is becoming very serious.

I have just seen that, owing to the labor shortage, the regulations forbidding the work of women below the surface in coal mines are going to be withdrawn in the central provinces.

There is very little personal news—just routine life.

August 8, 1943. Ahmednagar

There is a mild Empire boost going on here. Our Weekly Commentary—for the exclusive use of the Services of India—on July 29 prints an article by Sir Norman Angell, who "puts in true perspective the real import of that Empire." Here are some of the brighter gems produced by this ass: (1) "If there had been more of imperialist exploitation in, say, the West Indies, there might have been less of poverty, and the British taxpayer would not today be handing out large sums for the relief of colonial budgets." (2) Under British rule India has built 42,000 miles of railroad, which have enormously diminished famine by quick carriage of grain. (3) India's irrigation system is now the greatest in the world—over 30 million acres are irrigated in the country as a whole. (N.B.—Out of a total of 233 million acres cropped area in 1934, or 12.8 per cent.)

But it is the same as with religion—the facts are there, and it is facts which mould the actual lives of the people. Let our imperialists boast of their Pyakara Dams and Lloyd Barrages—never will any of us who have come to India for this war forget the unbelievable, indescribable poverty in which we have found people living *wherever* we went, and in millions. We are all agreed that if the people back home knew of these conditions there would be a hell of a row—because this state of affairs is maintained in the name of the British. And yet, too, we are agreed that there is no parallel, no common visual or verbal symbols that could convey the slightest understanding of this state of affairs to the people at home. How can I tell the people of Nine Elms that their condemned houses are palaces compared with Indian slums? They just wouldn't believe me—would think me a liar. At home one is shocked if families live in one room. But how often do people from India explain that millions of human beings here *have no room at all,* that whole families live in *houses* made of plaited grass, rags, bits of tin, a bit

89

of carpet—in all not more than 8 ft. by 4 ft., and perhaps 4 ft. high. And one can see this not only in *every* village, but on the outskirts of every town before one ever reaches the brick-built slums in the center of the town.

The new slogan is "Unite against Congress for a stronger British Empire." But the fundamental weakness of the whole policy was expressed by Amery himself when he said: "In many cases, as in that of wheat, measures of price control had to be reversed owing to the difficulty of securing the necessary *physical* (N.B.!) control of the commodity." What an admission! In a country where almost the whole population, every organization, is demanding control of prices and punishment of hoarders and profiteers, the Government confesses *physical* helplessness!

But hunger does not wait on governments, neither do hungry people respect correct policies or politics. Thank goodness life is materialist. It really would be ghastly if the essence of reality were to consist of the contents in a dispatch from our official reporter, Colonel As-you-were—who displayed such traditional gallantry in the eighty years' war against the aborigines, and whose son is now broadcasting from Berlin on his favorite theme, "liberty." Life has *its own* news bulletin, thank God.

August 13, 1943. Ahmednagar
Today I was called into the office to see our Colonel, who told me he would not allow a letter I wrote you at the beginning of the week to be sent, and gave it back. He was very nice about it.

August 20, 1943. Ahmednagar
I have this week been bothered by an upset inside—I refused to go sick as I have a grand lot of lads in the squad I am instructing, and didn't want to miss a single day with them.

The most interesting news from India comes from Bengal—in particular Calcutta. It is reported that during July 622 prosecutions were instituted in Calcutta by the police and inspecting staff of the Civil Supplies Department on charges of hoarding and profiteering during July, as against 174 in June. And an editorial in the *Statesman* comments and asks what is the use of prosecutions if the punishments meted out are so small that the profiteers don't worry.

90

The *Times of India* reports that on August 18th 129 people were picked up in Calcutta off the streets in a state of collapse due to starvation, and the next day the number picked up was 182, making 445 in four days.

People's Food Committees and unofficial Relief Committees are still on the increase.

Tata and Co. has given Rs.50,000 towards free food kitchens. The Calcutta Chamber of Commerce have opened five free food kitchens, and in a public statement blamed the Government for exporting rice. You will understand quite clearly Tata's motive, Nobel (armament manufacturer and multi-millionaire) *Peace* Prize.

One important fact to be noted—train-loads of grain are being taken to Bengal, but are obviously not reaching the people who need it. Incidentally, on July 25th, the leader of the Bengal students (who have been doing magnificent anti-fascist work among the peasantry) was murdered at Mymensingh. At Dacca, on July 23rd, another leading student was severely stabbed and is dangerously ill in hospital. On August 2nd three more students were attacked and seriously wounded. The fifth column has resorted to murdering the patriotic students because of their work among the people.

. . . This letter is a very tedious one—to tell you the truth, my repeated visits to the office make it difficult to write just as I feel— every sentence has to be thought out before it is written, "letting I dare not wait upon I would." There are such tremendous events to write about that one just cannot fill pages with "I am all right. Are you all right? It's all right. That's all right. Love and kisses." Life just isn't like that.

August 28, 1943. Ahmednagar

In my last letter I gave you some of the details of the famine in Calcutta. The number of starving people picked up in streets were: August 21, 46; August 25, 43. But be clear on the fact that Bengal, *as a whole,* is like this.

Recently, in Delhi, a Government spokesman in a food debate gave a long list of how every effort made to get food to the people of Bengal (import, transport, purchases, anti-hoarding, etc.) had been openly opposed, hindered, ignored by the *local officials.* Now the Mayor of Calcutta is reported to have sent a telegram to Churchill: "We appeal to you in the name of starving humanity to arrange for immediate shipments of food-grains from America, Australia and other countries." But the *fact* is that there is enough food in India now. Appeals of this kind by the Mayor are only the cover—as is the excuse that the army is eating everything to incite the people against the army—the cloak to hide the hoarders, the big grain merchants, the landlords and the bureaucrats *who have engineered the famine*—as the bridges of the Marne were left for the German army.

The points that must be grasped are: (1) that the standard of living of the Bengal peasantry is in normal times so low as to make the engineering of a famine an easy job to any bureaucracy; (2) that this bureaucracy, the landlords and petty tradesmen, are richly endowed with fifth column elements; and (3) that things are bound to drift until the Government end this policy of deadlock, which can be very much helped by the release of Congress leaders on condition they tackle the food crisis (a positive future condition, instead of the backward negative condition of repudiation of the previous years' struggle).

What to do? I consider it would be of vital importance to the war effort if the people in England demanded the immediate sending of foodships to Bengal—the food to be taken over by the Food Minister, Srivastava, and through him to be distributed by the *voluntary food distribution organizations now springing up everywhere*. Also, a vigorous demand for *real* punishment of those convicted of hoarding and profiteering and the immediate arrest of all provincial functionaries who obstruct or have obstructed the Government food instructions.

While I cannot discuss military questions, I would like to make it clear that the Bengal situation can only hinder operations, it cannot affect the outcome of the war with Japan. But it is now laying the foundation for a horrible mess after the war—besides all the unnecessary suffering now.

September 5, 1943. Ahmednagar

In India our chief item of news is a demand of Rs.3,000 security by the Government from *People's War* for publishing articles about the Kayyur comrades who, although facing execution (now carried out), appealed to the Indian people to unite against Japan.

All over India there is a stirring to meet the situation in Calcutta and Bengal. Relief Committees, food diversions, etc., etc. In Calcutta for five days—August 29-September 2—484 starving people were taken into hospitals. Dead bodies are picked up in the streets —in ten days, up to August 24, amounting to 155. It is estimated by Government there are 80,000 destitute in Calcutta, of which 40,000 have come in from the countryside. I am certain people in England could do a lot of good by raising their voice in demand of immediate rationing throughout India; price control of all food grains; heavy punishment of hoarders (the big ones), profiteers and incompetent (?) officials. I am certain a demand for a food ship from Australia to starving Bengal would be of the greatest value both from an immediate practical food point of view and as a concrete counter-blast to the propaganda of Bose and the Japanese.

Of course, with the famine has come cholera—140 cases in seven days, August 14-21. I am very well aware that India is the problem of Indians—the Indian people have got to learn politics just as we have got to—for instance, it is now becoming clear to the people that the Moslem League Ministry in Bengal consists itself of some of the largest hoarders, i.e., Pakistan, as understood by the Moslem grain merchant and a Moslem peasant, means two different things. But in the meantime *we* have our responsibility to make friends with whom we can. If we don't do this, we have not learnt the lesson of Dunkirk—the military defeat was obvious—but still more important was the fact that there was *not a single nation* willing to come to our side—we were only saved because Hitler attacked the East and Japan Pearl Harbor.

September 10, 1943. Ahmednagar

Today a curious thing happened to me. Twice fellows had spoken to me of a rumor that I was soon going back to the regiment. So this afternoon I approached my troop captain for information, since it affected me. To cut a long story short, it follows from an interview I had over a previous letter, in which I expressed certain despondency. At the time I explained I was fed up for lack of work and because we were not getting on with the war. Ap-

93

parently this was taken to the Brig *with* those papers which follow,
me round. It was decided to send me back to the regiment—
which decision has been O.K.'d, and H.Q. notified Gunnery Wing.
But now we have plenty of work, so the Major is now asking to
keep me on as he cannot afford to lose instructors. So for the
present I am still to be here—but I will let you know future
developments.

On Monday next I get a new squad, let's hope it turns up O.K.
—I am just beginning to feel I know something about our tanks
and guns—one more squad will give me full confidence. Should I
be sent back then to the regiment I shall at least go back knowing
my job pretty well. When I do get back I shall move heaven and
earth to get a thorough D. & M. training. But all this talk about
going back is in the nature of trying to plan one's life rather than
just pure drift.

Two interesting statements have appeared recently about the
social content of the Bengal famine. The *Statesman* says, "the
vast majority of the destitute are dependents of landless laborers
or those engaged in allied occupations. In many cases the family
has disintegrated under the stress of economic conditions." Recently
a letter appeared in the *Times of India* in which the writer explained
that these days the landlords would not accept rent in kind but
insisted on money.

Last night I had a very pleasant surprise in an invitation to a
special Indian dinner at my artist friend's house. So I shall have
to hurry to the station, for I would not miss such an invitation for
anything.

September 14, 1943. On leave in Poona

I am writing this in the sitting room of the Sergeants' Mess,
Poona Leave Camp. But to begin at the beginning, I had a most
delightful lunch with my artist friend. His brother, a doctor, was
on a visit to give him treatment so I was invited to meet him. His
wife and wife's mother served us. We sat on wooden seats about
2 ins. off the ground. The meal was in a room just off the kitchen.
Of course we had taken off our boots, etc. Each had a large
Indian silver plate with the various ingredients of the meal put
round the edge. A small metal bowl of what they call buttermilk

took the place of water. A pattern, done with vermilion and white powder had been drawn on the ground. In front of me was placed a little silver stand in which a stick of incense burned. Nana's elder daughter also ate with us. The whole affair was so very civilized and friendly. Afterwards some friends came round to meet me but I had to leave to catch a train.

We had a good journey and arrived at the leave camp where we were received—welcomed would be the truer word—by the Sergeant-Major. This place is really a vast improvement on the Willingdon, etc., clubs.

The *Times of India* reports 132 starvation cases admitted to two hospitals on September 11th. But in the statement giving these figures appears the following explanation: "Death in the majority of these cases was due to chronic ailments and diseases which had been neglected in the past." The fact of the matter is that now, after the publication of figures and photos and as a result of these, the whole of India is being roused, furthering National unity. The Bengal Ministry—who without question harbor in official posts members of the fifth column—are now getting wind up and beginning to suppress the figures and make excuses.

Months ago I write to you of the famine conditions in Bijapur District. Yet it is reported, "Distress continues. 60 relief works in progress. More rain urgently needed. 63,374 persons on relief works. 65,191 on gratuitous relief. 15,981 at the free kitchens." Belgaum District—distress continues. Satara District (Targaon taluka)—distress severe. From Lahore comes the report—"Cholera has broken out in an epidemic form in the Attock district."

These three facts are of interest: (1) Wheat stocks supplied to the Government of Bengal at twelve to thirteen rupees a maund have been sold at as much as twenty rupees a maund; (2) Sir Edward Benthal asserts that 30 to 36 wagons of food daily are being sent from the Punjab in the direction of Bengal; (3) Sir Chhotu Ram, Punjab Minister, and well-known pro-hoarder sympathizer, has asserted that "the Government of India were able to transport only 62,000 of the 218,654 tons placed at their disposal by the Punjab Government in July."

The thing that stands out a mile is that the Government showed no signs of weakness when it came to the arrest of the Congress *in glaring contrast* to its utter helplessness (??) (or should we call it cooperation, tie-up) in the face of the grain profiteers (and in a similar situation—the cloth merchants—the coalowners, re employment of women underground).

While the political resolution at the T.U.C.* was a vast step forward, we must be more concrete: (1) Release the Congress leaders; (2) Send food ships from Australia immediately; (3) Arrest and severely punish the grain hoarders and cloth profiteers; (4) Arrest and severely punish the officials in the Bengal Administration; (5) Give official recognition everywhere to the People's Food Committees. A National Government is not now the current link. The immediate necessity is to allow the Indian patriots liberty to fight famine, profiteering and the fifth column. Liberty to India is not a formal question but a very personal one.

Acute shortages of rice are reported from the town of Madaripur, Kuirgram in the district of Rangpur, Muktagachia in the district of Mymensingh, and at Pabna.

In Dacca, 168 cases of starvation were admitted to hospital between September 4-10. Corpses are being picked up daily from the streets and the Municipality has appointed a special staff to do the job.

In Noakhali, there is a severe shortage of rice. A shop-to-shop search is being made by the district magistrate himself today, while batches of sub-deputy magistrates are making house-to-house searches for hidden stocks. (But it is only the little people who get searched—not the big merchants in the Punjab and Calcutta.)

After strolling up and down the only two streets we're allowed in, for God knows how long, I bought a book *The Hindu View of Art,* by Mulk Raj Anand. I was moved out of the bookshop by the police—out of bounds to British troops. The idiot informed me that there were plenty of other good bookshops I could go to. There are certain things in this life which are so obvious, so everyday, that one never thinks of recording them. But I am certain

* In September, 1943, the British Trades Union Congress adopted a resolution calling for the release of all political prisoners in India, and the formation of a National Government on a free vote of the Indian people.—*Ed.*

future generations, even possibly the next generation as a whole, will look back at our epoch as a complete blackout of the human intellect.

These last two days we have had some sun, it has got much warmer. The flowers are magnificent, and one sees the most elaborately patterned butterflies.

September 15, 1943. On leave in Poona
Today I picked up three different papers. From the *Times of India* comes the news that on September 13th, 150 cases of starvation were taken to hospital. Forty-eight people among the starvation cases died in hospital. A leading article says: "Calcutta is but a symptom. It has its roots in rural Bengal. The cases of starvation come from the rural districts. They are landless laborers unable to secure rice at the present price. Conditions are not very much less serious in Bihar and Orissa. Bijapur is an earlier casualty but the malady persists. Famine-like conditions prevail in the ceded districts of Madras Presidency. Malabar is also afflicted."

The *Pioneer* (Lucknow) of September 14th gives the following information. In Chandpur, 103 sick and starving persons are undergoing treatment in local hospital. One hundred unclaimed bodies have been collected from the streets and disposed of by the Municipality. In Cuttack, the Orissa Merchants' Relief Committee has issued an appeal in which it is stated that in Ganjam district there have been nearly 330 deaths since the middle of May due to food shortage. A small paragraph says that 1,455 deaths occurred in Bihar from cholera during the week ended August 28th out of a total number of 2,480 cases.

I see that Australian Labor has passed a resolution demanding the re-opening of negotiations between the British Government and Congress. This is good, but in my opinion it is also too formal an approach to the Indian problem. Because in fact the issue is not between Congress and the British. The issue is between the Indian people and the present rulers (including the large hoarders and profiteers). I am convinced that the practical proof of sincerity of the Australian and British peoples is the sending of food ships at once with the demand for the immediate release of Congressmen

97

so that the food sent may be distributed by the people's food committees.

Gandhi's description of peace in India—"It is the peace of the graveyard"—was never more true that it is today. A vast and ignorant bureaucracy holds down everything and everybody except the means of oppression. I give details of the famine areas, not because they are outstanding but because they are the next shallow step down from the normal existence of millions of humanity here. I have never in all my life seen such mass poverty, never believed it possible. It is ghastly. That is why the demand for food ships is important—we have got to establish some *human* relationships, as distinct from correct political resolutions, between the British people and Indian masses. Any scoundrel can shake hands with representatives of the 4th Indian Division—what is wanted is a recognition of the elementary *human* needs of the Indian people. To hell with abstract politics and abstract art.

In one way, by far the most encouraging news is a report from Bombay that 300 Congressmen and women back from jail met at a tea party in Bombay and considered the present situation and what work could be undertaken under existing conditions. While reiterating their confidence in Mahatma Gandhi's leadership they decided to take constructive work of the following kinds: Food problem; Hindu-Moslem unity; Civic grievances; Relief for National workers and their families; Labor organization, student organization; women's organization, etc.

As I have said before the continued retention of Congressmen in jail is simply aiding the food crisis. Indian patriots must be given freedom to act—and not merely formal freedom. And since army units were employed in the round-up of Congressmen there is not the slightest reason why the army could not take a hand in arresting the large hoarders and profiteers. Such an action would strengthen India's war effort immeasurably.

There is a "Grow more food campaign" on. What enthusiasm can there be for such a campaign when everyone knows that huge foodstocks are being held and enormous profits being made by the big dealers and their friends in the Government? Accusations and counter accusations are being made—but what is needed is that the people's food committees should be allowed to investigate.

98

Last night I got back from leave in Poona. There is very little news from India or from me personally.

The main news is not at all pleasant because of a new turn in the position—one does not know as yet how far it will go. The background persists—Calcutta, September 15th, 198 starving cases taken to 3 hospitals. 56 deaths in hospitals. September 16th, 196 and 39. But now reports are coming in from Chittagong, Madairpur, Serajgunj, Jalpaiguri, Comilla and Dacca. It is from this last place that the first reports have come of looting. Four hundred maunds of rice looted from a house—300 men took part. The *Free Press Journal* gives this detail: "The stock which belonged to a firm of contractors had been seized by the police and was kept in the custody of the firm." On September 16th, 30 maunds of rice were looted from 100 maunds on the premises of the City Relief Committee. Five hundred men took part.

The Press during last week gave these bits of information: Prof. Vakil, University Professor of Economics, Bombay, said in a lecture, "taking into account the loss of imports of rice and additional requirements in the country due to the war, the total food deficit might be put at not more than 50 per cent." It is reported that the Sind Government have, as a result of the recent drive to unearth rice stocks, offered further surpluses for export of 10,000 tons of rice and 12,000 tons of paddy. Of Chittagong it is reported that the rice position is worsening and stocks have disappeared following the recent control order—there is a scarcity of sugar, although stocks are said to have been distributed to the local dealers.

I again give you these facts to show how very serious is the situation—that it shows ugly signs of developing from people peacefully dying of hunger into food rioting—which, of course, is just what the fifth column wants. *The point about this is* that the police (already) and maybe the military will be used against the starving people *instead* of rounding up the large dealers, government officials, etc., who are responsible for the famine. It has to be realized that Calcutta has no rationing, that Delhi is thinking of introducing rationing for Indian cities *next year*.

The ordinary, decent people in England *must* do something— this is *their* Empire. I have no doubts about our beating the

Japanese in spite of the state of India; but what fills me with horror is the post-war payment we shall have to make. It is all very well to parade members of the 4th Indian Division around England —but the sincerity of that praise wears a bit thin if those men's relatives are dying of hunger in the villages of Bengal and elsewhere.

One thing should be noted about the Calcutta figures. The deaths I have reported are of those who died in hospital. Such deaths from August 16th to September 16th were 752. But dead bodies picked up in the streets between August 1st and September 17th were 2,195.

September 24, 1943. Ahmednagar

I enclose in this letter a page of notes from papers *re* the famine in Bengal. I have not included any of the ghastly stories now appearing from time to time in the press as I don't want to be accused of propaganda—what I send you are just facts. But there is one fact that no newspaper prints—that millions upon millions in this country live on the border-line of starvation *always*. Their poverty is too dreadful to describe. I insist on this *fact* because it is in the long run the basis of the present famine—the smallest dislocation from normal produces famine.

There is a big difference between such a state of affairs and that of a people being so accustomed to a hard life that they can withstand some calamity. Year after year of living underfed, *appallingly* housed (if one can use the word to describe a tent-like structure made of rags, bits of matting—floor space 4 ft. by 8 ft. and maximum height 5 ft.—in which a whole family shelters in monsoon, cold and heat, the smallest children without clothes at all) and gaining a livelihood by scavenging, doing sweepers' work in the filthiest places, etc. Such communities are to be found outside every village or town. In speaking of them, one is not speaking of the slum dwellers whose standard of living is "higher." Millions upon millions of poorest peasantry—ill-fed, uneducated, down-trodden—patiently accepting their hideous lives only because they cannot see any way out. This immense abuse of all human decency by our British Imperialists—all this is taken by Halifax

100

to mean that there is "popular support for our way of governing India!"

I will not harp on this theme any more—as they say, "facts speak for themselves," and even while dead men cannot speak, their rying can be heard.

From September 16th to 22nd, 1,435 starving people were admitted to hospitals in Calcutta, where 365 died. These are by no means the total deaths, as is shown by the fact that deaths in hospitals from August 16th to September 18th were 860. Dead bodies picked up in the streets from August 1st to September 18th were 2,364.

The *Times of India* reports from Silchar that hundreds of famished and destitute men, women and children from southern and eastern Bengal have arrived and more are coming here daily. "Most of them live on the roadside. Thin and weak from lack of food these people—looking more like animated skeletons than human beings—are moving from door to door in the hope of getting some morsels of food. During last month about half a dozen bodies were removed from the trains on arrival here." Similar news comes from many other places.

I have now done one week with my second squad of B.O.R.s—they are a grand lot.

I have just seen that the number of destitute people being fed daily in relief kitchens in Bengal is 820,269.

September 28, 1943. Ahmednagar

The news of the setting up of the India Relief Committee in England is really splendid. And today is published also the resolution and donation of the South Wales Miners. This is even better.

But it is extremely important to make clear to people at home the significance of the following. In a speech Srivastava, the food member, said: "Bengal's population was 60 million; her main crop, rice, was reported to have yielded in 1942-43 about seven million tons and there was a carry-over of 1.7 million tons from the previous year. Under the original basic plan it was agreed that a supply of 350,000 tons of rice from outside would place Bengal on an even keel. This quantity worked out to a little over 5 per cent of the normal production of Bengal." He went on, "Is

101

not one entitled to infer that a good deal of Bengal's own production is not available for consumption?" Again it is reported that in Bogra, rice was not available in the town for the past few days following the prosecution of some dealers.

Yesterday the *Statesman* published the weekly deaths in Calcutta—August 29th to September 4th, 1,183; September 5th to 11th, 1,292; September 12th to 18th, 1,319; September 19th to 25th, 1,492—compared to an average for previous five years of around 570. From Dinajpur, Haniganj, Dhubri, Rangpur, Bogra, Kuhlna, Feni, Silchar, Sylhet, Jessore comes the same ghastly story.

But on September 27th, the *Statesman* published a report of food rioting in Jammu Kashmir. Four people killed. The next day a long report appeared—seven killed (two more died later) and nine injured when police fired on a violent mob. Twenty-five policeman and officers were also injured. Curfew has been imposed and the military are patrolling the city at night. I warned you of this development in my last letter—but I did not expect it in Kashmir.

There is one thing that must be explained—it is admitted everywhere that there is just enough food *in* India now to feed the starving millions—that food is going to Bengal, but is *not* reaching the masses. Two things must be done. One, the arrest and punishment of the big dealers, the kings of the black market, the big hoarders and the immediate confiscation of their stocks for free distribution to the landless peasants, the small peasants and the poor townspeople in the famine areas. Two, the immediate sending of wheat to India to make posible the use of all available stocks *now* to feed the hungry and at the same time give the Government a basis for meeting future needs. But merely to send food now without the severest punishment being meted out to the vile criminals in high places—just because they donate thousands of rupees to the war effort funds—is *not* saving the starving but spreading the cause of the famine, i.e., the power of the profiteers. This is the only program to solve the crisis, and Congress must be set free to secure the cooperation of the people.

Let me put the matter in this way. India is ruled, is run in the present way, in the name of Britain. Then it is time every decent human being in Britain demanded immediate changes in the state

102

of affairs. *We* are the rulers in India—if India suffers from famine under *our* rule then *we* are responsible to the starving peasants. We have no right to claim to be rulers here if at the same time we don't punish with the utmost severity those swine who for profits, or any other reason (even if they do "support" the war funds) spread and deepen the distress of the masses.

The other day my name was on Orders—War Substantiated Sergeant, meaning I cannot have my three stripes taken away without a court-martial. In one sense this is really nothing to be proud of because if the war can be dragged on long enough I shall automatically end up field-marshal. But, on the other hand, I have got where I have without in any way altering the conditions which prevented me being made a Sergeant at Perham Down two years ago, and of which I was reminded so strongly only the other week. I have heard no more about becoming an officer—but *how* I have enjoyed being with my two squads of B.O.R.s.

This letter contains little personal news—my whole mind is so concentrated on the poor people here—if only I could really *do* something about it except write letters. And it fills me with horror when I read of the military being used against the starving people instead of against those bastards responsible for the famine.

October 2, 1943. Ahmednagar

There are various excuses for the famine given by interested persons here—one could list them as follows: (1) The army is starving the people to eat itself—origin, the Fifth Column; (2) British rule—origin, the Japs and the Fifth Column; (3) The loss of Burma—origin, the bureaucrats and the war-mongers who long for their properties in Burma to be recaptured; (4) The small farmers who won't release stocks—origin, the big grain dealers; (5) The *other* party or the *other* province—origin, political gangsters such as Huq, late Premier of Bengal. But now a new line is appearing in the main from England, thus:

"The famine in Bengal . . . is at once a consequence of the incompetence of the Indian administration of the province to grapple with the situation and of the greed of Indian speculators and hoarders who have endeavored to make money out of the misery of their own people."

103

It is important to consider this question of the Indian administration. A year ago took place the arrest of hundreds of Congressmen in Bengal, including 20 members of the Bengal Legislature. The Huq administration in Bengal was therefore left high and dry, and became so incompetent as to warrant Huq's dismissal by the Governor. Then followed the present Moslem League ministry. By sheer force of necessity this ministry has had to carry out some measures, to recognize some established facts—i.e., people's food committees, etc. But at Calcutta and Howrah nothing is done. Big business called a halt and found certain Ministers willing to cooperate with them in profiteering. Bengal today is not an example of Indian administration but a glaring result of the suppression of Congress and the consequent extended freedom of political gangsters.

The famine spreads, and now the demand grows for Section 93* to be applied, i.e., the bureaucracy to take over because the Ministry has failed. In the name of efficiency the friends of the big grain dealers will become dictators—the big grain dealers themselves having produced the famine and obstructed relief and rationing.

Whatever happens, *we must not fall for this.* I see that Sir J. Maynard wants a Food Dictator. That is not the solution. What is wanted is the release of Congress, the mobilization of the people to organize relief—and the use of the police, with the military if necessary, to arrest and shoot the hoarders and confiscate the hoarded food. We claim to be here to defend India—then let's get to work.

News of the famine situation continues, which is by no means confined to Bengal. Orissa is described in the papers as a "land of flood and famine."

A report from Ganjam says: "Malaria is raging in an epidemic form in the coastal villages—thousands are going without any of the usual food. Their food is mere grass, some roots or some leaves."

From Dacca it is reported that no rice or other foodstuffs have been available in the city for the last 15 days, and that rich and poor are starving and dying by hundreds. From Comilla it is reported that rice has disappeared from the markets of the town, and

* The Government of India Act, Section 93, gives powers to the Viceroy and the Governors to take administration completely in their hands.—*Ed.*

destitutes roam the streets. The same story in many towns. Cholera is also breaking out.

Re the Jammu shooting which I told you of in a previous letter, a women's deputation has met the Premier and impressed on him the urgency of suitable action against the Jammu police, who, it is alleged, made a ruthless lathi charge on women. The Jammu Bar Association is making representations also, stating that the Jammu situation was mishandled by responsible police, and the firing was indiscriminate, ruthless and too prolonged, and demanding an independent inquiry.

The issue here—a most vital one for India and Britain—is: Do we want the people to starve to death quietly and so leave everything to the profiteers? Do we want the people to resist starvation? And if the people protest at *being made* to starve, do we want the police to shoot at them? Or are we going to restore order by arresting the profiteers, by confiscating their stocks, and by helping people's food committees to distribute the confiscated food to the starving poor? Just how do we want things to be run? Or are we going to drift to worse confusion and increased hatred for us by the Indian people?

October 5, 1943. Ahmednagar

When I got back from the Ranges today, I was told by the Major that I was being returned to my unit on Monday next. I shall refrain from comment or explanation at the moment. Anyway, I have learnt a lot of gunnery; I have met some more Indians and my last two squads of B.O.R.s have been a great joy. What will happen next I don't know—one has to get used to this sort of living and make the utmost use of all circumstances.

October 10, 1943. In the train

The whole affair of my leaving Ahmednagar is a repetition of my move from the 54th to 57th Tring. Regt. It has had the usual result of teaching people by what happens under their own noses, something that you and I know very well.

Last Friday there was a dance at the Sergeants' Mess. I turned up late, as I had had a previous engagement to meet some Indians for a discussion—which was grand, as usual. At the dance—it might almost have been a farewell party for me—several sergeants tennis. But what was really exciting was the sudden appearance of Kelkar, my artist friend. He had got a note I sent him, and so was determined to see me. He brought with him the enclosed little photo of his family, and a painting, which I will send you. I promised to see him this morning, early. When I got there I had a very touching reception. He explained that the whole family had wept when they got my note, and that he had been determined to see me again. We had some coffee and fruit. They then gave me some cakes, made by his wife for my journey. We went from his house to a photographer friend, who presented me with some lovely photographs. He also took my picture, for, as Kelkar explained, "I want to have your picture so that my children will always know of their good Karkar (uncle), a real friend of India." After which I got back to barracks to do all the necessary kit expressed the view that the whole affair "stank." But what was rather amusing was the attitude of the officers. One, whom I had never spoken to in my life, came up and said that he had "hated reading my letters." Another invited me round for a drink and a chat before leaving. They were all anxious to impress me with their individual innocence and put the whole blame on higher up. But you see, it so happens, that I know from remarks made that my views were discussed amongst them. Officially it is being said that "his regiment wants him back." Whichever way it happened in detail—the broad fact is that I am being sent away from here by those who are terrified at any real criticism of their way of living and ruling. And on the other side I was able to not only make friends among the Indians, but in *practice* show them that among the white sahibs there are some men who are not affected by color prejudices and who are really fighting for a new world.

Yesterday I was feeling rather fed up, so I played five sets of checking, etc.

I had a brief interview with our Colonel and Major—both stressing that my work had been magnificent and thanking me for what I had done. Then I returned to the bunk, where my little bearer gave me a small bunch of flowers and hung a flower-chain over my shoulders. When I got into the truck the driver said: "Your bearer says you are a very good sahib—you never got angry when he made mistakes and you always smiled." So to the train.

Finished on arrival.

. . . The beginning of my journey was quite interesting. After leaving Ahmednagar we went through miles of sugar-cane. Two passengers explained the following facts: There had been a famine in these parts, so the Government built the railway and irrigation works as relief measures. Now the area produces a fine sugar crop. So business men came from Bombay, built sugar factories for sugar extraction and thereby forced the sugar-growers to sell to them at the manufacturer's price—so the peasants are still poverty-stricken.

But the last part of my journey was like a nightmare. The endless view of plains, crops, and small stations, turned almost suddenly into one long trail of starving people. Men, women, children, babies, looked up into the passing carriage in their last hope for food. These people were not just hungry—this was *famine*. When we stopped, children swarmed round the carriage windows, repeating, hopelessly, "Bukshish, sahib"—with the monotony of a damaged gramophone. Others sat on the ground, just waiting. I saw women—almost fleshless skeletons, their clothes gray with dust from wandering, with expressionless faces, not *walking*, but foot steadying foot, as though not knowing where they went. As we pulled towards Calcutta, for *miles,* little children naked, with inflated bellies stuck on stick-like legs, held up empty tins towards us. They were children still—they laughed and waved as we went by. Behind them one could see the brilliant fiendish green of the new crop.

Part III: Address Unknown

Thank goodness I am back with the unit. In every way it is better than Ahmednagar—I am in the pink, very happy to be back among the lads, and always hoping we can get on with this endless war.

October 28, 1943

The deaths in Calcutta for the week ending October 23rd were 2,155. The death-rate is increasing in the rural areas. Mrs. Pandit,* President of the All-India Women's Conference, gives an account of her visit in Midnapore. She states that the rations given out at the food relief kitchens are so small as to be hardly worth giving, that medicines to counter malaria, cholera, etc., are practically non-existent, that the bodies of the dead can be seen everywhere—decomposing, eaten by vultures and dogs, floating in canals, etc.—that whole villages have been deserted.

I am incredibly fit—I am also very busy with my crew, getting my tank absolutely tip-top. Quite by accident—actually while out in a truck to get showers—I learnt something of the *feudal* condition of India. All round our camp are the usual fields, peasants working, farmsteads with tiled roofs, tin shacks, etc. About a mile away is a vast building with a huge brick wall all round and a road leading to the entrance. I asked the driver, "Is this a prison?" It reminded me so much of Wandsworth or Pentonville—its high wall pierced high up with a row of little windows. "No," says he, "it's the palace of the Maharaja."

One thing about the famine that has got to be watched. The Bengal Government has a scheme for rounding up the destitutes into shelters, where they will be fed and clothed and, when ready, sent back to their villages. Now this is an "improvement" on the existing practice of picking up a destitute, even taking him to

* Nehru's wife.—*Ed.*

108

hospital, getting him recovered, and then putting him back on to the streets. The new plan means, in fact, sending these starving, landless peasant laborers back to the conditions which are the very source of the famine.

It must be stressed that the cure of this famine is not the immediate feeding of the people from outside, but some real wide changes in the methods of production and land ownership—i.e., back in the villages work and food must be found—not along the old basis of relief works (the method in Bijapur, where there is still famine after a whole year) but on a permanent basis of financial aid to the peasants (loans, tax relief by cancellation and reduction, organized provision of seed for next crop and land distribution, and, above all, to raise actual production, the introduction of machinery for deeper ploughing). One of the many things which hits one everywhere is the complete absence of modern machinery for agriculture, although India already possesses the Tata steel works. Of course there are greater experts on this kind of thing than I, but my meaning is, "don't think the famine in India can be cured by charity."

November 1, 1943

This is to send special good wishes for Christmas. I know you agree with me that a little less wishes and a little more deeds would bring about the Peace on Earth we so much want. One cannot help thinking at this time of the year of the people in Europe who, allowing no excuses and overcoming all obstacles, are actively fighting the enemy. I sincerely hope that sometime soon my own prisoner-like activity may end.

Today we have had a day off, so I went for a walk with two friends. In my last letter I mentioned that nearby was a Maharaja's palace. We went to the gate and asked if we could look round, as we were interested in Indian architecture. "Certainly." So we walked through the grounds—unfortunately we could not go into the house (a very large building like Knowle) as the "King and his family were living there." But still we saw some interesting stone carving over the gates and main fronts of the palace—huge designs of branches and leaves—very heavy and deeply carved. A lorry gave us a lift back to camp.

Everything is now a complete secret—only the chai-wallahs know who we are, why we are, etc. So you see I cannot write much.

Three nights ago I went, after work, into the town. I bought some cotton underclothes, and had a very good meal at a restaurant, of which there are dozens, with prices extraordinarily low. I was walking down the pavement when I heard a child crying, sobbing her heart out. I went up to the noise—it was dark—and saw a little girl lying on the pavement edge. So I got out some annas and knelt down to give them to her and spoke to her.

Some Indians collected round, and I asked one of them what was the matter with her. He replied, like a statistical fact, "She is one of the starving children." At that I lost my temper completely, and told them they should be bloody well ashamed to walk past a child in her state. I made some of them take the little kid to a relief center. The whole incident upset me so much that I cannot face going into the town again, because being in the army I don't know what I can *do* to help these creatures—it is not good enough just looking at them with sympathy.

Yesterday I went down the road to get some clothes mended, when ahead of me a small party of little boys came down the road shouting something. They were carrying a flag. As it was quite dark, I had to go close to see which flag. It was red, with a hammer and sickle on it. I asked them, "Are you in the Y.C.L.?" The answer was most unexpected. "We were Labor Party, but now we are Bolsheviks." I bought a copy of their paper—and have learnt a little more about Indian politics and Indian people.

I am now in Calcutta. Last time I came here, for miles and miles along the railway lines and at stations, there were starving people. Now there is not a sign of famine—*it has been organized with the ability of genius.* The deaths in Calcutta hospitals have dropped sharply—71 on November 9th, 69 on November 6th, with only 134 admissions.

But from Munshiganj it is reported that deaths among the destitute are not being recorded in death registers maintained by the Union Boards, as particulars of identity are not obtainable. It is feared that fishermen class Kaibartas and Risbis are going to be extinct in many places.

In the *Hindustan Standard* it is reported that in the week ending November 5, 267 deaths occurred in Chandpur town and in the 53 unions (groups of villages), on an average more than 200 *in each.* The report states: "Almost all the dead bodies were thrown into the 'khal' and paddy fields—to be devoured up by dogs, jackals and vultures—as there was no man available to bury or burn those corpses. From Comilla an outbreak of cholera is reported. Dead bodies have been found floating in the Buri river in the Muradnagar Thana area," says the *Hindustan Standard.*

The point is that out in the villages people can starve to death without anyone knowing about it, while on the basis of the falling mortality rate in Calcutta Amery will no doubt claim that the famine is over.

In the *Amrita Bazar Patrika* appears a letter from Mrs. Ela Reil, Provincial Secretary of the All-Bengal Mahila Atma-Rakeha Samity.* "We appeal to the Government to stop the forcible repatriation of the destitutes, which has had the following effects: The destitutes have become panic-sticken . . . they are hiding, where they die of hunger, since they dare not venture out for food . . . mothers are torn away from their children, husbands from wives. . . ."

In the same paper appears another letter from a Calcutta resident: "I witnessed this on October 30: A motor-van suddenly came in the locality and the men came down and dragged the destitutes into the van . . . at which there was a great uproar and confusion, and the poor, helpless destitutes ran pell mell and looked for shelter wherein they could take refuge. About 30 or more forcibly entered my compound and hid themselves in the outer staircase of the house. When, however, the motor-van taking a good number of them disappeared, the poor fellows came out in the street again and began frantically to search for their kith and kin."

In other words, the starving people are now being *driven* away from Calcutta.

Now on all sides it is being openly admitted that the amount of food given at the Free Kitchens is so very scanty that a hungry man

* All-Bengal Women's Self-Defense Committee.—*Ed.*

cannot live on it. Also, everyone is agreed that the transport problem is acute—is it not obvious then that to get grain to the villages is going to take even longer? From Manikganj the secretary of the Hindu Mahasabha writes: "Provincial Hindu Mahasabha kindly allotted 500 maunds of rice for this sub-division. It was booked on the 20th of October and reached Rajari on the 22nd, but up till now the rice has not been sent to Galundo by the railway authorities on some pretext or other. The wagon is lying at Rajbari station for five days together. . . . The number of deaths every day in the sub-division has reached three digits and cremation and burial being out of the question, dead bodies were recklessly thrown into rivers and canals." (*Ibid.,* November 9.)

The Bengal Relief is now distributing some sort of clothing to the poor wretches.

One of the social changes being brought about by the famine is an enormous sale of small properties, which means that the ever-growing number of landless peasantry has increased even further. The actual feeding of the starving has hardly begun, and no permanent solution is possible without radical land reform.

I am very fit, but I can say nothing of myself as a soldier because of the necessity of secrecy. All I can say about it is that it is going to be tough. Before anything happens I would like to know the Red Army has driven the fascists off Soviet territory and even more, I would like to hear of the opening of the second front. But the future is ours.

November 21, 1943

Personally this week has not been over exciting. We had a good surprise pay-out on Saturday (Rs.75) so I decided to give Rs.55 towards the Famine Relief. I went down town and after a scout round found the right place to give the money. I feel a bit happier although I wish I were in a position to do more. I do what little I can—mainly in the direction of explaining to other fellows about the famine—specially arguing against the serve-them-right and shoot-them-all-off theory of the regular soldier.

One chap with whom I had a terrific argument came and told me that while down town yesterday, a small boy asked him for some bukshish, so he took him to an Indian cookshop "to see if

112

he was really hungry." The little brat ate *ten* choupatties (like pancakes). This impressed T. so much that he has repeated the story many times.

Last night I had a good time in a coffee house—I got into conversation with two Indian fellows and had a good discussion on India. As usual the discussion turned around the question, "How can it be explained to Indians that the British are allies when the British soldiers refer to us as black bastards and treat us so badly?"

It is very difficult to write these days as everything of importance has to be left out for fear of giving away military secrets.

November 29, 1943

I am sitting on the grass outside a long army hut. Not far away is sitting an African Negro (as anyone will explain "just out of the jungle—they'd be much happier with bows and arrows") reading a book. Five minutes ago a B.O.R. came up, stopped, and said to him, "Can you read?" "Yes." "What's the book? *Miss Blandish?*" "No, *Pygmalion.*" I just had to record this—whole books could not present the present world situation better.

The newspapers report that the coalfields in Bengal and Bihar have been exempted from the regulation which prohibits the employment of women underground. The cause of the present coal shortage is given as "shortage of labor." The press note says that certain stipulations have been made regarding the employment of women and that "special efforts will be made to ensure the welfare of women employed underground and a woman welfare officer will shortly be appointed for this purpose."

It is unnecessary for me to make any comment except that there seems to be no limit to which the bloody Government of Delhi will not go to antagonize and degrade our allies, the Indian people. But, of course, one must keep in mind that the Indians are incapable of self-government so we must maintain our "trusteeship" and show them how it should be done. I have often said that the more I see and learn of India, the more I am reminded of Tsarist Russia, and the more certain I am of the outcome.

Yesterday I went down town and round the bookshops, and found my way in the end to the Friends of the Soviet Union where there was quite a stir on my appearance as there were two "special branch" visitors in the room. I bought a copy of the *Indo-Soviet Journal,* with an excellent article by Joseph Needham in it, and retreated in good order. I then went to a restaurant where I had a long discussion with the waiter who is a convinced Congressman. He was very like some others I have met—devoted to Gandhi and Nehru as *Indians*—ignorant of world affairs—hating the British with a burning hatred which gets more and more confirmed by daily facts around them. To him, a pro-war anti-fascist policy meant support for the British. In the end, he very solemnly apologized for talking like he did to a man in uniform—it was very good to have an argument with a man like that.

We shall be moving again soon. Today the Padre asked me if I would help to produce a unit paper—of course, I said yes—it should be interesting.

. . . Today I went again to the coffee house, and this time got in conversation with some Indian students—we had a long discussion on the significance of the English poets Auden, Spender, Eliot, etc.—a grand evening. My introduction to the special branch at the F.S.U. was but an incident—it appears that the Police Commissioner has now informed the F.S.U. that in future "special branch" men must be present at *all* their lectures. I see in the paper that Conservative M.P. Ferris has made a study of Indian affairs, and has delivered himself of the profound judgment that India is not ready for self-government. I wonder how many whiskies and sodas it took to produce such an original conclusion.

December 2, 1943

I have met some very interesting people these last two days. Two Bengali writers, and yesterday evening the grandson of a famous Indian doctor who died recently. The lad is still in his teens, but judged by our English standards, very precocious. Yesterday I wrote an essay on the position of modern English poetry—especially Auden, Spender, etc.—by request of a friend to whom I had given a verbal account. I have also met an old acquaintance from Acton so we had a good talk.

Last evening I had a really grand time. I met Professor Sen, the principal of one of Calcutta University Colleges—he himself was at Cambridge 30 years ago—he is a distinguished mathematician. We talked in the main about the lack of facilities for British soldiers to get to know educated Indians. After seeing him, I had a long talk—more of a lecture (and very interesting) on Indian art of which he had some examples on his walls— with the editor of a magazine called *Modern Review*—an expensive journal like the *Geographical Magazine* with articles on economics, art, world affairs, etc.

I am told that my notes *re* British poets have been made up into an article for publication in Bengali. Every experience I have had out here bears out the fact that Indians have a tremendous respect for cultured Englishmen—in this respect there is not the least trace of hatred as there is for the imperialist—they speak with most profound gratitude of the work of the English director (I have forgotten his name) of the Calcutta school of painting who virtually re-awoke Indian artists to Indian art. I have been promised that when I come back here I shall be taken to see a very famous Indian artist.

It is December 4th and we are again on the move. It is nearing zero hour. One cannot say this and this are the things I am thinking of, except perhaps a concentration on clothes—darning, buttons, vests, socks and pants, etc. All day I have been sewing clothes and in general preparing for the job ahead—trying to get every detail arranged, underclothes washed and so on.

I will post this letter as soon as I can, as of course I don't know what is going to happen next.

Always remember that one is given by fate only one lifetime in which to work and live for humanity. There is no greater crime in my opinion than to renounce the world, no matter for what excuse. If anything should happen to either of us, never say, "It is finished." For we have both lived for one purpose, the emancipation of the working people. If by chance one of us has to leave this work before it is done, then let the other go on and see it through—not in the spirit of holy self-sacrifice—as a monk or a nun—but even more in the fullness of human experience. What we miss we can only find in knowing humanity more deeply and not in the ever narrowing circumference of private memories. Life for me has only been worth while in so far as I have been able to show, even a few people, the way to *forward* living. And above all, whatever happens, let us never for one instant, on the slightest excuse, forget we are human beings and belong to the brotherhood of man. Tyrants and hermits are tarred with the same brush. Whatever happens you must go on *living*—there are so many years of grand work ahead.

December 6, 1943

I wrote this poem last night, called "Orders for Landing":—

> Today we got our orders for tomorrow
> A few brief sentences as a title page
> Preludes a book. Each one wonders how
> The story will turn out. What's over the edge?
>
> Yesterday, far as memory spreads back
> The shifting incidents of daily life,
> Lies at our feet, where we stand upon the deck
> Always moving somewhere—self away from self.
>
> It is I who move. I who will look again
> To find the I that searched and could not see
> Exactly the I that am. Had I but taken
> I as the recurrent particle of continuous We!
>
> There's no unknown to him who reads the sea,
> For whom the horizon predicts the certain land.
> Like words we live, self-lost in history.
> We sink like waves into the endless end.

December 14, 1943

We are now allowed to mention a number of things which I did not do before owing to "military information." We are now quite close to the Japs. We were visited by a *Very Important Person* in our jungle hideout. It was an entirely different show to the one of over a year ago—he did no inspection, sent the officers to the back, gathered us all about him and gave us a little personal review of events.

I went for a short walk on Sunday morning and as usual pried into any empty peasant huts I came across. Here they are built on exactly the same plan with the same type of mud stove, the

116

same earthenware pots, same methods of hanging utensils from the ceiling. By far the most interesting thing was a large room about 6 ft. 6 ins. high with a few heavy ceiling beams carved with various designs which were colored—one of the designs was made up of two *muskets*; if I get the chance I will make a drawing from these. Their huts are walled with palm matting which in the place of the usual muddy walls makes them really quite pleasant and airy and light. Whenever I go into these villages I have a great desire to have some place like a museum for houses where one could see, if possible, historical examples of houses of the common people instead of the usual palaces, temples, etc. You and I have enjoyed what we call the picturesqueness of the country cottage— it is something which one takes for granted and one does not realize is an artistic expression arising out of generations of what one might term "handicrafts," part and parcel of the most intimate life of the peasants.

Life here glides by like a falling leaf, so that very often I don't know either day or date—but I always listen to the news. This morning I had a walk through the woods—very lovely and so English—or, shall I say, so peaceful? Please, when you can, give me the real reasons for the abolition of co-education in the U.S.S.R. —this matter is worrying me a lot as I can think out no satisfactory explanation.

December 22, 1943

It is still very difficult to write. Our Colonel gave us a lecture the other day during which he said, "I told G.H.Q. that if you were not used I would take my hounds away altogether; but I hope to get you blooded nevertheless." The phrases were familiar, but I could not help thinking of Fred* who also rode to hounds and had ideas about warfare.

It is quite astonishing what a lot of men received letters from home which spoke of the Mosley release—one can well imagine the feeling aroused.

I am keeping very fit and now enjoy quite often a good wash down in a little stream near by—the bed is fine, clean sand—the

* Frederick Engels.—*Ed.*

117

sun is very hot and I am pretty sunburnt. But at night it gets pretty chilly with a heavy dew. The birds and butterflies are really beautiful. These last two days my crew have been building themselves a new shelter to live in—it will help to keep our kit and ourselves much cleaner.

It was stated over the radio the other day that the famine which ravaged Bengal is now officially ended. Look at my letter where I dealt with the clearing of Calcutta and you will find there a prophecy. Such statements must be taken with a pound of salt.

December 25, 1943

Today is Xmas Day. We are all making the best of it, but everyone is really "back home by the fireside." Last night we sat around a fire and sang songs. This morning we started with some tea with rum in it. At the mid-day meal we follow the custom of Sergeants serving out the food—though actually under active service conditions the exclusiveness of ranks is broken down normally every day.

It is now December 29th. Xmas Day ended with a very happy gathering of all my company round a fire. We sang songs, told bawdy stories, ate some hot sausages and peas and drank a little beer or rum and lime. One lad had written a poem especially for the occasion. I was asked to do a turn, and said I knew no jokes, but would recite them a bit of poetry about London, so I recited Wordsworth's "Westminster Bridge." Later on I was called on for a speech so I told them that in the hard days to come if they stuck together in the same spirit with which they had got together for Xmas we would do all right.

We have a regimental paper, *Bully-Tin*—I am on the editorial board. We had a meeting the other evening, after which I had a really interesting discussion with the Padre on Christianity and Communism.

Reports from various Bengal districts show that while famine relief work under official and unofficial auspices is continuing, the price of new rice is going up and the incidence of malaria and other diseases shows no sign of abating. Due to shortage of labor, harvesting of paddy has become very difficult. Acute shortage of

118

labor is being felt everywhere and is hampering the cultivation of winter crops.

Tomorrow we go on an outing which may be interesting.

Later. The outing *was* very interesting, but was spoilt by some fellows shooting a cow belonging to a little farmer and taking it away without paying him. I protested to my officer and Sergeant Major. We are supposed to be fighting for a new world and we are supposed to be the friends of the people and yet when we go among them we behave like a gang of thieves. It made me very angry. I shall try to raise the matter again.

> Jagged rocks jutting out towards the sea
> An ox skull white on the bleached sun-dry earth
> Dead wood once a forest giant-tree
> Rotted, worm tunnelled, nothing worth—
> All these time scatters along his path
> Round boulders smoothed by a stream
> dead . . . Like a peasant's bowl,
> A man's head buried in his place of birth
> Millions of years old.

January 4, 1944

I have just seen ι little fish colored black and yellow, like a wasp —there are also other fish with horizontal lines for camouflage. Also a number of fish constructed very like a lizard—a very long body which is curled up when they rest on the sand or on a rock. I have not been able to get close enough to see whether under the fins there were legs or just two stumps. It is staggering what one can see here. I have found butterflies with a similar pattern on the wings as our peacock butterfly and the case above of the Zebra-wasp-tiger-fish camouflage seems to hint at some law of coloration. I have come across a common creeper with purple flowers the leaves of which are in pairs. The color when old is gold-yellow —when fresh a green which goes golden when the sunlight shines through them. This creeper is the hunting ground of a yellow-gold butterfly whose wing shape is exactly the same as that of the leaves . . .

119

I am on guard again tonight and it is very cold. This last few minutes I have been writing these lines:

Millions of years old—over the whole
Hangs the universe like a dome
Pillared on mountains, that fade into their own height,
Breaking through dense jungle-shade to white,
And higher yet into the burning night,
Star-spluttering and belching darkness.
Over the whole spread a silent vastness
So still, the silence recoiled on itself
And broke to pieces in a myriad whispers—
A mountain stream worming its way to the sea—
The hushed shifting of sand before the breakers,
Heard from miles beyond the forest's edge—
Insects' wings brushing the breathless air—
A leaf falling on leaves and the drip of dew,
Then through the night the howl of homeless dogs
To hurl the stillness back into no noise.
When from the hills, not seen till touching the trees,
Morning, like a flock of flamingoes, wings
To settle in the branches and spread across the fields.

January 8, 1944

I have been all day on small arms firing. It meant four walks through woods. During it I saw a butterfly—a deep velvet brown with a streak of pink gray—the exact color of white sunlight on brown—this business of light imitation is remarkable.

An interesting little social incident is taking place here. We are in a rice-growing area—small peasant cultivators. The area was cleared of inhabitants for military reasons. Now that the rice is ready, the peasant men are allowed to come in during certain hours under armed escort. The peasants will only gather their own crop, which is often as much as ½-mile from the road. They have to go over a mile along that road to get out of the prohibited area. The result is each man collects as much as he can possibly lift, and jog-trots the distance. He does this as much as four times a day,

120

with the result he is absolutely exhausted. Orders are to shoot anyone who is not out of the area by the stipulated time (a necessary precaution against fifth column) and also to drive on stragglers. I need not comment on the whole business, but it is the living result of poverty, plus peasant ownership, plus imperial army. One Indian was crashed into by a motor-bike. Another, given a warning shot to hurry along, collapsed. Some of the sahibs encourage the work with sticks.

Once more we are moving—we leave at night, and one cannot help but reflect on how, to the thunder of Dinosaurs and Ptero-dactyls, man crept from the primeval forests to new horizons (poetic licence, as in fact he left much later at the time of the woolly rhino and sabre-toothed tiger). I must post this letter this evening as there may be little chance of writing a letter for some time.

January 16, 1944

From now on my letters will consist of scraps of paper written at odd moments during the coming compaign. We are only a few miles from the front line, and yet see very little signs of war—an occasional distant barrage—a few aeroplanes and yesterday A.A. puffs chasing a Jap machine. As to my own feelings—very rarely I feel a tinge of fear, plus regret—in the main I worry about whether I shall command my tank as a Communist ought. I only hope I shall do the job efficiently. I am keeping very fit—in spite of being many years older than most of the fellows, I can still do everything they do, except run—there I am beat. One of the lads is making a grand meal for this evening out of some rations we got yesterday—a sort of feast.

My gunner, Monte, has just got back from a trip to the forward area—what has most impressed him is that while the British and Japs shell, mortar and bomb each other, cattle continue to graze on the battlefield and peasants with children work on the road and farmsteads. Another thing—he came across five graves of British soldiers, with the only mark a beer bottle stood up on it—no cross, etc.—the fellows, on hearing this, all said it was a fine sign of good spirits and just as good as any other tombstone. I may go up with a party of commanders to have a look tomorrow.

121

I am in the very best of health and very happy. I am now a Troop Sergeant, and the lads in my troop a very good crowd indeed. Yesterday I got a chance copy of *Soviet War News,* with an excellent article *re* co-education in the U.S.S.R. The whole business is now quite clear and *very* encouraging. Zero hour is getting nearer, and although I am by no means a superman, I cannot help feeling glad that I may do just a little bit towards beating fascism. The lads have just cooked some really superb raisin fritters—God knows where they got the ingredients—flour, butter, raisins, milk, baking powder. I got four copies of October's *Daily Worker.* It was grand to read it again.

We are now only a few hundreds of yards away from glory. "There are those who would like to philosophize on the question of sacrificing space to gain time." You will remember the reference. But even so, it is still rather like a mad hatter's picnic. We make our beds down, we sit around and chat, we sunbathe (not so openly as before) and we sleep. While overhead scream mortars, etc. To this, and all other incidents of war (such as A.A., Jap planes, our own barrage, etc.), the lads react with "Ignore it" or "Quiet!" and just carry on sleeping, reading, etc. But I must say one thought runs through my head continually—Spain. Here we have such complete mastery in armament of all kinds! What holds us up are the Jap entrenchments in the numerous small foothills along the Mayu range. These hills are most peculiar in that they have no rock or stone in them, but are like piles of sand— harder than loose sand but softer than sandstone—the Japs just tunnel on a larger scale to the way children make tunnels in sand castles.

The whole hillside is covered with thick shrubs as much as ten feet high. An important point of the shrub is the large quantity of extremely prickly and tough-fibrous bushes—as good as any barbed-wire—which the Japs also use to cover paths. I might add these "paths" are just tracks through the undergrowth, leaving all top surface of elephant grass, leafy boughs, etc., untouched so that they are invisible from outside. I give you this description to show you the really appalling job it is for the infantry. In any appreciation of this campaign the character of these natural earthworks has to be understood. I estimate a platoon of fit men could in a week or so make such a fortress, and there are dozens of these mounds (they aren't hills, not even as big as Sudbury.) Their great weakness is the softness of the sand and the isolation of either single hills or small groups.

This morning a party is going to watch some strategic bombing—I am sending two others of my crew on the principle that the more each man knows of the landscape, the better in every way. The bombers are just coming over—we climbed up on our tanks to have a grandstand view of 12 Liberators and dozens of Vengeance dive-bombers exterminating the Jap positions at Razabil cross-roads. Now that the bombers have gone there is a real barrage of small stuff. This may be the solution of the Burma problem. Now I am ever so excited to hear the reports of what was the effect. It may seem strange to you that in a sort of way I cannot help gloating over the affair—it is the reverse of Spain a hundredfold.

February 4, 1944

Last night I posted a letter covering our first action. The lads in my crew made up a good hot meal, after which we sat and talked for a long time. This was the first evening since we moved from here that we were able to fix up our inspection light. Beforehand I went to visit B. and asked him what he thought of the battle. "All right. Bumper says our main job is to convince the infantry that they can safely go to within 20 yards from the targets we're engaging, so accurate is our fire."

After all we had a dry night, and from the look of things I hope we shall get some sun to dry our kit. Breakfast is up.

. . . This morning we cleaned up the tank, made ourselves more comfortable and prepared for rain, and did some washing. One fellow caught a snake about 18 inches long—green on top and just behind the head a salmon pink. Rumors are about *re* our next move, but nothing definite. I have just seen what may be the smallest moth I've ever seen, white, with blue-black markings on wings and light brown head. I must get ready for a tank commanders' lecture.

123

... I am feeling rather down in the dumps this evening, for two reasons—the food is so bloody unappetizing—and we have been warned that our next operation is going to be more difficult—which means far more responsibility and physical strain (I was pretty well on my chin-strap at the end of one day), but perhaps one will get used to it.

... Today a V.I.P. is turning up, so we have to be in overalls, boots and berets, instead of our usual shorts and stripped to the waist. We've had it—all lined up—"How long have you been in the army? Always in this regiment? How long troop sergeant? Find things all right in this country?" And in everyone's mind is one thought—they want to get on with the war instead of asking useless questions. After the "do" we recalled all the Generals we had been inspected by, and then listed those who inspected without warning of their visit.

At 1:45 there is a parade, when our C.O. is to speak to us; it should be interesting—he is a splendid officer. I heard a crack during mealtime: A. This bastard stew! B. What are you kicking about? You never had food like this in Civvy Street. A. No, I didn't, not even on a Friday!

Later we were reminiscing about games we'd played and seen. My driver, who had been quiet all the time, suddenly chimed in: "The only team I ever played for was the street team. I was in reserve. We called ourselves the Primrose Juniors. Whenever the other side got rough the reserves were called up. It always ended in a scrap." He comes from Glasgow and is broad as he is tall, but with quite a baby face—an *excellent* lad.

... As I predicted, the Colonel made an excellent statement, and cleared up a lot of misgivings. Apparently in the battle we caused a considerable number of Jap casualties in men, sufficient to affect the outcome of the campaign. I cannot say how soon I will be able to write again. I enclose a sonnet I wrote a day or so ago:

> Where light breaks up obscurity for sunrise,
> And peace accumulates the parts of storm.
> Where death's the sequence of the pregnant womb
> And embryo contains the adult's size.
> Where mountain peaks hold up the moving skies

Their might is tunnelled by the invidious worm;
Where clouds pile up their cumbersome white form
The flat laborious plain of wheat-fields lies.

Women and children build up the only road
Where overhead the shells of death whine past
And cattle graze indifferent to the din.
I felt perhaps I'd understood at last
By close observance of all that nature showed
"When life has gone, then where does death begin?"

A Letter from Indian Friends

Calcutta, April 25, 1944

DEAR MRS. BRANSON,

We are sorry to write to you on such a sad occasion, but hope you will allow us to share with you the sorrow which is terrible and heavy.

Some of us had the privilege of knowing your husband, Clive Branson, when he was here in Calcutta. It was necessarily a brief acquaintance, but we came close enough to know and feel the man that he was, and the valuable friend of the Indian people that he always had been. He was with us the evening before he left for the Front, and he was the same cheerful and kindly comrade who looked forward to seeing us on his return. Our sense of personal loss is further deepened by the feeling that our people in particular is poorer for the death of Clive Branson. We shall remember with sad gratitude that he was one of the first to die in the defense of our country and die for our cause, the cause of the Indian people and the people of Britain and the world.

We can do nothing more than offer you our heartfelt sympathies for the loss which is yours—and ours, too, no less.

We remain,

CLIVE'S INDIAN FRIENDS

LaVergne, TN USA
30 December 2009
168599LV00003B/101/A